Wicca For Beginners

Everything You Need To Know About The Wiccan World Including Basic Knowledge Of Spells, Moon, Herbal, And Candle Magic. Starter Book To Practice Witchcraft

Antony Vithale

Antony Vithale

THIS BOOK INCLUDES:

THE BEGINNER'S GUIDE TO WICCA

Candle, Crystal Magic, Herbal, Moon Spells And Wicca Spells

WICCA BEGINNERS GUIDE

A Wonderful Guide About Wicca, Including Symbols, Instruments, Spells, Rituals, Celebrations and Festivals

WICCA FOR BEGINNERS

The Ultimate Guide To Wiccan Beliefs And History, Magic, Witchcraft, Candles, Crystals, Runes, Herbs And Magic Rituals

TABLE OF CONTENTS

THE BEGINNER'S GUIDE TO WICCA

WICCA BEGINNERS GUIDE

WICCA FOR BEGINNERS

Antony Vithale

THE BEGINNER'S GUIDE TO WICCA

Candle, Crystal Magic, Herbal, Moon Spells And Wicca Spells

Antony Vithale

INTRODUCTION

A re you new to Wicca? I used to be too. So was each of the over 1.5 million Wiccans out there, according to a Pew Research Center study in 2018. It is true that being a new Wiccan or Witch comes with a lot of mixed emotions, which may include uncertainty, nervousness, fear of rejection, ignorance and panic, among others, on the one hand, and feelings of optimism and hope for the attainment of a new and fulfilling spiritual plane, on the other hand. Therefore, it is not surprising that if you are a potential Witch or have just begun your path in Wiccan practice, you find yourself in such a dilemmatic situation where you harbor doubts about the sanity and wisdom in your decision. This is normal. The truth is, whether you were born into a Wiccan household or not, you are bound to have those feelings at the time of your decision because of the nature of Wicca: occult, esoteric and relatively new. With a population of less than two million people spread across Europe and other parts of the West in their small covens, you are likely to find few if any Wiccans who make their faith public. Owing to this, you are most definitely going to have doubts and entertain fears. But again, I tell you that this is normal!

Based on the foregoing, so many questions have been asked and answered over the years about the nature and practice of Wicca by different categories of persons such as religious scholars and students, inquisitive individuals, members of other religions, and, more importantly, potential and beginning Witches, who will form my target in this book. No doubt, the questions are endless. As I guide you through the concept, I'll unearth some more salient questions and address them promptly, all in an attempt to gratify your curiosity, help you in the decision-making stage if you're still hesitating, and establish your feet in the religion as a Wiccan novice. Regardless of which category you fall into-student, potential Wiccan, or beginning Wiccan, this comprehensive book aims to provide answers to all your questions, but more importantly, it is intended for all new Wiccans to serve as a reliable guide as they embark on this valuable spiritual path.

For a start, even before we go into all the details I have packaged for you in this book, it is necessary to briefly hint at the nature of Wicca as a religion and a set of practices. Wicca is often described as an unorganized religion, as it has no designated place of worship, lacks a central sacred text, and there are no generally accepted standard ritual procedures to observe. All of these details are better decided by individual traditions, covens and solitary practitioners. Despite this flexible nature of the Wicca religion, one very important element of the Wicca religion that serves as a structural center for the religion is the *Wheel of the year*. The Wheel of the Year is the term used to describe the body of festivals and celebrations in Wicca. Various festivals for diverse purposes make up the Wiccan Wheel of the Year, and they are all significant to the Wiccan experience. In other words, they are quite important to you as a Witch. An important dimension to each of these festivals is that typical of every Wiccan activity, they can be done your own way! This is the height of individuality in Wicca. It emphasizes *me* over *us*. There is no binding regulatory organization that controls the practices in Wicca! Shocking, right? There are more revelations about Wicca that will interest you as we press on in the discourse. Brace up!

Like every other neopagan religion, Wicca is essentially polytheistic in worship. What this means is that Wiccans believe in more than one supernatural being or deity. It is the belief in Wicca that the Goddess is the most fundamental deity on which the religion is founded. The Goddess is the god of life and fertility, but as life cannot be individually given, especially via reproductive means, the Goddess is aided by her ally, the God. Based on this hierarchical structure, the Goddess is superior to the God. Typical of the nature of Wicca, there is a divergent belief from this. Some Wiccan groups believe in the existence of the Goddess alone. This monotheistic perspective is not without its basis. Such groups believe that Wicca is one of the answers to the world's quest for a female deity, and some scholars are quick to defend this by drawing a similarity with the Roman Catholic deification of the virgin Mary. This leaves us with the reality that a supposed neopagan religion could be monotheistic. This is yet another interesting feature of Wicca. In addition to the Goddess and the God, there are the smaller deities that also play key roles in the Wiccan spiritual hierarchy. As a new witch, this is a key component of Wicca in which you must be versatile, to get the best out of your Wiccan experience. In a subsequent part of this book, I dedicate a full section to the deities in order to help you understand your relationship with them and how well you can interact with the supernatural beings in order to bring to fulfillment all your personal Wiccan goals. In addition, it is important to touch on the magical dimension of Wicca at this point, as it is undoubtedly the reason why many potential Wiccans or new witches choose to join the religion. The practice of magic, sometimes spelled as 'magick', is predominant among Witches, but this is in no way to imply that all Witches practice magic. Owing to its popularity among Wiccans, many have come to understand magic as a primary and indispensable component of Wicca. To put it most directly, this is not true. As a matter of fact, magic is optional in Wicca. It is one of the ways by which Witches bring to reality their heart desires. Care should be taken not to mistake the Wiccan magick with the everyday magic done by illusionists and tricksters for commercial entertainment. The Wiccan magick has far more spiritual significance than the common illusions you see on the so-called magician's stage. Magick involves spiritual spells, rituals, divination, communication with unseen spirits and gods, and so on. To accord it some supernatural weight and magnitude, some Wiccans choose to address their magickal activities by the term 'witchcraft', or simply 'the craft' and, again, this requires some differentiation because of the negative connotations that have ensued from it. For your sake, as a newbie, I shed some more light on this confusion in a later chapter. The most important thing to keep in mind at this point is that, regardless of whether magic or sorcery is important in Wicca, the decision to deploy your magical powers rests solely with you. Another similarly important foundational issue to iron out as you prepare to launch into this book revolves around the term 'Witch'. Who is a Witch? Who is a witch? Is a Wiccan any different from a Witch? Are Wiccans allowed to practice witchcraft? I could go on and on with the questions drawing from the endless questions I have encountered in my practice as a Wiccan scholar and from my encounter with people who, like you, are curious about the subject. To put it in the simplest form, a Witch is a person who believes in the practice of Wicca as a religion and a guide in their spiritual journey. A clear distinction should be made between the term 'Witch' with the majuscule initial letter and the term 'witch' with its minuscule counterpart. The word 'Witch' is the term by which believers in Wicca are called. In other words, it is a title for everyone who decides to take up the Wiccan Faith. It must be said, however, that not all Wiccans like to be called Witches. Some would rather be called Wiccans because of the negative implications associated with the other title. You will find a more detailed discussion of these two related but very different terms as you read on. I must say in advance that what you have in your hands is a complete package on Wicca that could serve as an encyclopedia on the subject. You will find clarifications to your doubts, explanations of the fundamental Wiccan beliefs and practices, and, more importantly, enough information to guide you through as a new Wiccan hoping to grow and establish your feet in the religion or an intending one as the case may be. It is my belief that by virtue of your encounter with this book, your Wiccan journey will assume a more meaningful dimension. Make yourself comfortable and let's get started!

CHAPTER ONE.

WHAT IS WICCA?

UNDERSTANDING THE FOUNDATIONS OF WICCA

The first time I called myself a 'Witch' was the most magical moment of my life.

Margot Adler

Misinformation and misrepresentation are not far from Wicca. No thanks to its highly occultic nature and emphasis on individuality. It is bad enough that such misinformation has given rise to so many misconceptions about the neopagan religion so much that some religious scholars, members of other religions and the public at large consider themselves authorities in the discourse of Wicca. As a result, so many half-truths and complete falsehoods have over time made the round and have come to be consolidated as beliefs among members of the public. The situation is further compounded by the fact that Wicca has grown into many traditions and covens over the years with lots of variations in beliefs and practice, so much that there are very limited areas of agreement among the Wiccan covens in existence. Notwithstanding, the purpose of this chapter is not to lament the situations that have culminated in the diversified opinions and beliefs but to establish the foundational truths about the religion. I, therefore, advise that you keep your mind open and liberal enough irrespective of what you already know about Wicca.

WHAT IS WICCA?

Typical of its nature, Wicca has been subjected to multiple definitions by different categories of individuals across time and space. Whatever the perspective is, a few key points are worthy of mention about Wicca because they appear to be universal facts. First, Wicca is a modern neo-pagan religion or set of spiritual practices that can be traced back to Gerald Brousseau Gardner, a British civil servant who lived from 1884 to 1964, a period in which he was exposed to various occult beliefs and magical practices during his career in Asia. According to Thea Sabin, Wicca precedes the birth of Jesus, although not then known by the name 'Wicca', and it combines both traditional and modern practices such as dance, spellwork, rites, reverence of nature, belief in magical powers, annual festivals and celebrations, among others. Generally, most Wiccans refer to their practices as witchcraft, but this is again different from the conventional sense of witchcraft. Unlike most religions that emphasize the afterlife, Wicca focuses on the present life and revolves mainly around the earth, nature, life, sex, love and death, all of which are elements of the physical body, hence it is called an earth-based religion. In fact, Wiccans believe that life after now will be on earth and not in any heaven or hell as other religions preach. The earthly nature of Wicca is not, however, without a scientific anthropological basis. Sir Edward Taylor propounded in his 1871 book titled *Primitive Culture* that Wicca traces to a group of ancient men and women who believed in the superiority of the natural environment over every other realm. They viewed themselves as contemporaries of the environment in which they live — the trees, plants, flowers, animals, rocks, rivers, and so on, hence they treated these natural creations with reverence. More so, this belief matured into the Wiccan belief that although the Goddess and God are supreme deities, they manifest in humans, animals, plants, insects, and every other natural thing in the environment. Hence, they revere every natural element, believing that every natural element is sacred since the Divine is present in them. Based on this, you could come across a Wiccan or a set of Wiccans who tell you that their religious practice is centered on the worship of nature. The reason is not a mystery anymore! True to its eclectic nature, what started as Wicca in the 20th century has undergone a series of alterations over the years. It seems that every individual or coven or tradition through which Wicca has passed made sure to leave their signature on the religion either by adding to or removing from it. Or how else shall we account for the growing differences in beliefs and practices of Wicca? As a matter of fact, there are hardly any two covens with exactly the same Wiccan beliefs today. A major instance is in the theistic nature of the religion; is it monotheistic or polytheistic? Well, Wiccans will tell you that it depends on you! However, you would be on the wrong side to assume that this would elicit confusion. Far from it! Let's view the situation from the perspective of a small old tale I know. A set of blind men were once asked to touch an elephant and describe what they think it looks like. One of them touched the tusks and concluded that the elephant was all smooth. The one who felt the ears maintained that an elephant was soft all over.

For the one who touched the body of the elephant, it was flat and spread like a wall, while the one who touched the feet of the animal said it had coarse skin. Would you say any of them was wrong in their description? Absolutely not! This can also be said of Wicca. There is an unspoken respect for individuality among Wiccans. Wicca is a personal spiritual path to be walked by one person. Individual differences and preferences play a very large role. Owing to this, many irreconcilable differences in beliefs and practices have gained ground over time — differences that have resulted in innumerable covens and traditions!

However, lest you begin to develop the thoughts that Wicca could be confusing because of its many differences, I should be quick to mention that all Wiccan covens, notwithstanding their respective beliefs, are bound by certain foundational guiding principles which you should know as a new or potential Witch. They include belief in a supernatural being or beings, belief in the forces of nature and the natural elements, symbols, initiation, use of magical powers, reincarnation, the Wiccan Reed, and festivals, among a few others. Having so far discussed the meaning and nature of Wicca, it is high time we touched on its history in a bid to establish your knowledge on the foundations and development of Wicca.

HISTORY OF WICCA

As it is the case that no religion is without a historical and spiritual foundation, Wicca can be traced back in the 20th century to the teachings of Gerald Gardner and, specifically, to his works entitled *Witchcraft Today* and The *Meaning of Witchcraft*, published in 1954 and 1959 respectively. Prior to this time, Gardner belonged to a small group of witches, which he left to found his own coven with the aim of preserving Wicca. Note that the name "Wicca" was only popularized, not invented, by Gardner. This points to the fact that a certain form of Wicca, which was, of course, different from what we have today had existed before Gardner came on the scene. In fact, in its early days, what we know today as Wicca was frowned upon and dubbed *The Gardnerian Wicca*. Later in this book, I establish some vital differences between the ancient Wicca and the Modern Wicca. It must be mentioned that the increasing popularity that Wicca enjoys today owes to Gardner's expansion of the religion. He soon had his own disciples, one of whom was Doreen Valiente, who played a major role in the acceptance of Wicca in the United States around the 1960s. Widespread acceptance was aided by the feminist movement that embraced the religion because it worshipped a female deity. Little by little and in bits and pieces of dozens and dozens, Gardnerian Wicca began to spread. Its followers were initiated into small covens of disciples who were privileged to grow into priests and high priests who could found and lead their own covens. The multiplication of covens did not go without certain alterations in beliefs and practices as well. Covens began to determine for themselves whether they would serve the Goddess or both the Goddess and her God. Wiccans may simply honor a non-specific god and goddess or may worship deities of their tradition at their own discretion, whether it is Zeus, Odin, Osiris or even Apollo. In Gardnerian Wicca, the true names of the gods are only revealed to already initiate members and not outsiders. Wicca is distinctively feminist, and so they often consider the supreme manifestation of a deity to be a nature goddess. A major breakaway of this kind was what grew to become Dianic Wicca, a tradition founded by Alexander Sander, who was entirely feminist in orientation and based on Diana, the goddess of nature and fertility, which were the founding principles of Wicca.

On and on, and newer covens began to arise. Towards the late 1980s, the number of Wiccans who publicly admitted it in the United States and Western Europe had grown to over 50,000. Today, the number runs in millions! Thanks to the continuous rejection of Christian paternalism and the growing sensitivity to the environment. It could be said with a fair level of confidence that because of its highly individualistic orientation and eclectic nature, Wicca has changed a lot from what it was during the Gardnerian age. More and newer covens have sprung up with their respective variations in beliefs, rituals, practices, and lots more. It is no wonder then that it is difficult for these many covens to come under the coordination of a central authority or organization. **The Pagan Federation** and **The Universal**

Federation of Pagans are the only recognized bodies known, and they are largely ceremonial, with very little influence on existing covens and traditions. This notwithstanding, it is an unmistakable fact that Wicca has continued to grow in its reach, albeit slowly, and still sparks interest among scholars.

ANCIENT WICCA VS MODERN WICCA: THE POINTS OF DIFFERENCE

Whether Wicca is an old religion or a new one remains to date a point of argument among Wiccan practitioners and scholars, as well as non-Wiccans. As a matter of fact, Wiccans have had to doubt among themselves how new the practice is owing to its many similarities with the old pagan religions.

This situation has shaken Wicca from its foundations. Gerald Gardner, in the 1960s, had to claim ownership of the Wicca proposal, but this was met with harsh contradictions from witches who considered the practice to predate Gardner himself. Truth be told, Gerald did not invent the word 'Wicca' let alone the religion. More so, he was himself initiated into a certain Witch group before he seceded to form his own tradition. Witchcraft was already in existence and had always been a practice neutral of religion. In other words, anyone could practice witchcraft irrespective of their religion, and this is still the case to date. Why then do we credit Gerald Gardner with propounding modern or neopagan Wicca?

The answer lies in the peculiarities of Gardner's Wicca. I should also state upfront that although the Gardnerian Wicca is the most popular, there are several other versions of neopagan Wicca that developed over time, some of which are the Deboran Wicca, Alexandrian Wicca, Dianic Wicca, and the Thessalonica Wicca. Each of these groups has its peculiarities in terms of deities of worship and rites, among others but, together, they make up what we know today as the modern Wicca.

As I contrast the ancient Wicca with the modern, bear in mind that I do not refer to just the Gardnerian Wicca, but all neopagan versions of Wicca as a whole, since, despite their respective variations, their general worldview is the same. Discussed below are the major areas of difference between the ancient Wicca and the modern Wicca:

ORIGIN

It is only well-placed to begin this interesting discourse with history because it forms a very foundational stage in the debate between ancient Wicca and modern Wicca. How way back in time does Wicca go? It is common knowledge that Wicca predates Christianity, which has been in existence for over 2,000 years, but that is the ancient Wicca. The Wiccan practiced back in the Middle Age was rather remote, cult-like and hidden because of the stark rejection it suffered in the society. A certain British anthropologist and Egyptologist, Margaret Murray, described what was in vogue then as a pre-Christian religion called the Dianic cult in her works, significant among which are *"The Witch-Cult in Western Europe"* and *"The God of the Witches"*, which date as far back as 1921 and 1933 respectively. It is worthy of note that as at this time, Wicca had begun to undergo a series of changes but had not yet evolved into the Gardnerian Wicca. Recall that Gerald Gardner himself belonged to one of these witch cults having supposedly been initiated by Dorothy Clutterbuck in 1939. The ancient Wicca was highly totemistic and animistic and involved a belief in an ultimate personal God. One of the reasons Gardner's Wicca faced so many challenges is that he only changed the surface of the ancient Wicca and picked from several covens to form his tradition, which later grew to be accepted because he did not only popularize it but also passed it down to lots of disciples.

It must be admitted, more so, that what we know today as the Gardnerian or modern Wicca is a repackaged version of the older belief systems and practices. Although it is now essentially polytheistic, with one or two monotheistic covens here and there, the modern

Wicca still has traces of the ancient Wicca in it. Notwithstanding, the foundations of the modern Wicca are found in Gerald Gardner's works and activities. Afraid that the Wicca he had been initiated into would die out, he started his own coven, gathered several students and a new Wicca was born! Discipleship helped foster much of Gardner's version of Wicca. Aside from Doreen Valiente, his first disciple with whom he wrote books, there was Alex and Maxine Sanders who would later split off to form their own tradition called Alexandrian Wicca. There was also the American couple, Raymond and Rosemary Buckland, who spread the Gardnerian Wicca to the United States in the late 1960s. Raymond would also later start his coven called Seaux-Wicca. Another name worthy of mention in the history of modern Wicca is Sybil Leek, who is credited with the book *"Diary of a Witch"* based largely on the Gardnerian Wicca.

SUPERNATURAL BEING(S)

Another major area where the modern Wicca differs significantly from the ancient version is in the belief in supernatural beings or deities. Unlike the ancient Wicca, which involved the belief in a single personal God, modern Wicca is rather impersonal in its conception of God. It views the supernatural being as a genderless force, according to Raymond Buckland. This ultimate force is further manifested in the male and female deities known as the Goddess, which is also known as the triple goddess because it embodies the maiden, the mother and the crone, and the God, or in some traditions, the Lady and the Lord. However, some modern traditions do not buy into the idea that the life force is different from and is expressed through the Goddess and the God but hold that these two deities are at the highest level of supremacy possible in Wicca. In addition to the two ultimate independent deities are the smaller gods that operate immediately below the duo deities on the rungs of authority. Each of these smaller gods is believed to possess peculiar strengths that make it indispensable to its seekers. Different covens have their respective minor deities, which they place primacy on. Such gods are often kept secret and revealed only to members of the sect. Immediately below the minor gods are the spirits of the ancestors. Yes, it is true that when Wiccans die, they do not actually die, but only leave the present realm to become spirits and demi-gods who are powerful and can influence the lives and activities of those alive, and as a result, are consulted from time to time for protection, guidance, blessings, and many other purposes.

Typical of Wicca, the relationship of Wiccans with spiritual beings differ significantly. By 'relationship', I refer to the way Wiccans view and relate with God and the Goddess as well as the other deities and supernatural beings. Basically, Wicca is polytheistic, which is based essentially on the belief in the Goddess and the God, but as more and more covens have sprung up over time, they have diversified into many more religious orientations. Some traditions are pantheistic, meaning that they believe that God is present in everything in existence.

Note that this does not refer to the Christian God. According to Doreen Valiente in her book titled "*The Charge of the Goddess*", the supernatural being is quoted to say, "*Arise and come unto me, for I am the souls of Nature who gives life to the universe. From me all things proceed, and unto me, all things must return. And before my face, beloved of Gods and men, thine inmost divine self shall be enfolded in the rapture of the infinite.*" An interesting twist to the multiple orientations is that there is still the subtle belief that all the gods lead to one absolute force. It is like multiple paths that lead to one single destination. Every individual is encouraged to choose which path works best for them. Perhaps equally important to all Wiccans is the respect for nature and the environment. The reason for this is not farfetched — the founding culture of Wicca elevated the environment above all things. So, irrespective of their spiritual preference, all Wiccans are unified in their respect for and belief in nature.

THE SIGNIFICANCE OF THE NATURAL ELEMENTS

You can also call them classic elements. Generally speaking, the Wind, Air, Water, and Earth are the most basic factors required for life and fertility. As Wicca is based on these two, it is, therefore, no surprise that the religion largely depends on these elements in almost all of its practices. The only other one, Spirit, is a representation of the spiritual dimension of the religion.

But again, to think that the ratio is 4:1 further buttresses the emphasis of Wicca on nature and the environment. More so, they form the sources of life and are present in virtually everything with life ranging from plants to humans. They are the sources of energy that drive existence and are capable of both creation and destruction, although they function in their own way. It is these energy resources that Wiccans draw upon during rituals and festivals.

They do this by invoking each of the forces, facing the North, East, West, and South, which are believed to be the physical representation of the elements. This is referred to as **Calling the Quarters** and is completed with the invocation of the spirit element, which is summoned to the center of the circle. Sometimes, a Witch might choose to summon only an element or focus on one element because it is the element that can provide the force needed to fulfill the wishes of the Witch at that point in time. This implies that all the four classic elements and the ethereal element have their respective powers and functions, which I examine presently.

THE EARTH ELEMENT

The Earth element is symbolized by a triangle facing southwards with a horizontal line across it. Earth is home to all matter and represents growth and stability, and is essentially feminist. In addition, it provides material items such as money, security, sound health, and financial security, among other blessings. Deities associated with Earth include Pan, the Horned God, and Gaia, but behind these gods, Wiccans revere Earth a lot because they believe it is the home of humans, has been and will always remain so across many life cycles. During rituals, it is summoned for safety, security and especially for grounding.

THE AIR ELEMENT

The Air element is represented by a triangle facing upwards with a horizontal line across it. When you think of air, you think of freedom, but it signifies much more! It also represents knowledge, intellect, deep thought, travel and exposure, and so on. Air is masculine. It is naturally oriented towards the East. It is used in Wicca to develop psychic abilities, to sharpen the thinking capacity and to expose oneself to unknown realities. In Wicca, it is symbolized by items such as feathers, flowers, smoke, breath and so on. Deities associated with Air are Thoth, Shu, Mercury, and Hermes. Air governs the Witch's mental activities and allows for deeper insights into the supernatural realm.

THE FIRE ELEMENT

For Fire, the representative symbol is a simple triangle facing upwards. Some Wiccans prefer to call it the element of the sun, and that is rightly put. The Fire element is masculine and provides warmth, life, passion, and desire. The energy provided by this element ignites passion, energy, intensity and motivation, which could be both positive and negative. If harnessed well, the Fire element makes one passionate and charged to defy all difficulties in their spiritual journey. Some Wiccans also use it for purification purposes, drawing especially on its transformative powers to cause an effect on everything it touches. Associated zodiac signs are Aries, Leo, Sagittarius.

THE WATER ELEMENT

Water is symbolized by a triangle without a crossbar facing downwards. Typical of the flowing nature of water, this element represents the eternal movement of the soul and emotions. It is feminine, cold and moist. Some Wiccans consider Water superior to Earth because it has greater flow.

It is the belief that water has the ability to purify owing to its natural force; it clears off stagnation and releases tense emotions. Wiccans use the water element in rituals by pouring it over ritual items, using it in making brews and tossing objects into the water. Associated deities include Neptune, Venus, Tiamat, and Epona. It is necessary to conclude this foundational section with a cheerful note that the five elements are available to you at all times and can be consulted at ease. As you go deeper into the journey of becoming a Wiccan, you will find them continually useful at every stage. The next chapter will take you deeper into Wicca.

CHAPTER SUMMARY

Following a welcoming introduction, this chapter eases you into the basics of Wicca. It discusses the historical foundations of the religion and touches briefly on the five elements you will come across at every stage of your Wiccan journey.

CHAPTER TWO.

WANT TO BE A WITCH?

FINGERTIP PRINCIPLES OF WICCA YOU NEED TO KNOW

We do not worship the Devil nor do we believe in the Christian concept of Satan. We believe that to give evil a name is to give evil power.

Silver Ravenwolf

Every religion of the world encompasses a set of beliefs, dos and don'ts that differentiate it from others, and no, Wicca is not exempted from this rule system either.

It would be wrong to argue that because Wicca places primacy on individuality, it does not have its own superabundant beliefs and binding principles. On the contrary, it does. Irrespective of the tradition, there are certain most basic beliefs which are common to most, if not all, Wiccan covens.

This holds a vital implication for you as a new or potential Witch. In order to establish your feet properly and remain on the right path all through your spiritual journey, you necessarily have to become grounded in the most foundational principles revolving around Wicca. It is to help you achieve this that this chapter is written. If you must start, start on the right foot. Provided below are some of the most common beliefs and principles taught and practiced in Wicca.

NO RECOGNIZED HOLY BOOK

To start off with the most fundamental fact about Wicca, it is important to learn that if you are looking for a religion with dogmatic teachings and beliefs recorded in a supposed Holy book, Wicca is not for you. There has never been, and there is still no recognized official book of doctrines or teachings associated with any Wiccan coven. Owing to this, many religious scholars have argued that Wicca cannot be classified as a religion, but again, that is not a justifiable argument. As a matter of fact, more and more governments in Europe, as well as international religious bodies, continue to recognize Wicca as a religion, scripture or no scripture. The closest to a Holy book that can be found in Wicca is the Book of Shadows, which contains some religious texts and especially instructions for rituals. In some modern covens, the High Priest or Priestess keeps this book but is made available to members who would like to make handwritten copies for themselves.

NO EVIL, NO DEVIL, NO SALVATION

Another foundational belief in Wicca is that there is nothing like the Christian concept of a Devil whose stock-in-trade is "to kill, steal and to destroy", actions which they (the Christians) are quick to describe as evil. For Wiccans, Satan is nonexistent. In a way, this automatically cancels out the perception among non-Wiccans that Wicca is a Satanist religion because of its heavy involvement in magick and witchcraft. Witches do not acknowledge the existence of, let alone worship, the Devil. It is a mere Christian creation. A very important question; how does Wicca explain the negative incidents such as accidents, ailments, poverty, wars and many other sad events? These are mere natural events that occur to humans for the development of their souls. Raymond Buckland lent his voice to this assertion when he noted, *"It is necessary that the soul experience all things in life. It seems the most sensible, most logical explanation of much that is found in life. Why should one person be born into a rich family and another into poverty? Why should one be born crippled,*

35

and another fit and strong…if not because we must all eventually experience all things." In the same vein, Wiccans believe that there is no need for salvation as the Christians put it. This is because Wiccans do not acknowledge that mankind is sinful, and as a result, does not require salvation. In the words of Valerie Voight, "*We are aware of our own goodness and strength, and we are not afraid to admit it. We are not sinners and we know it. We don't have a Devil to blame our mistakes on and we need no Savior to save us from a non-existent Hell.*"

THE DIVINE BEINGS ARE SOVEREIGN

Wicca is more of a journey into the spiritual realm or a negotiation with the spirit world to bring about desired changes in the physical world than mere religion. This explains why it emphasizes a spiritual connection with supernatural beings. There is a fundamental belief that certain entities or beings operate in the spiritual realm in a hierarchical order. At the highest rung is the Moon Goddess. For Wiccan traditions that are monotheistic, this is their major deity of worship. The Goddess is responsible for fertility and gives life to all mankind and nature. For the duotheistic covens, however, the Goddess is aided by God to complete the fertility process and give life. After God comes the smaller deities, which are also believed to be capable of influencing the lives of their worshippers.

Note that the smaller gods are not in competition with the Goddess and the God in the hearts of Witches. Every Wiccan understands that the Goddess and the God are supreme and come first. The smaller deities may then be summoned depending on which ones you believe in. But that's not all about the supernatural realm. Souls of dead Wiccans are also in the hierarchy. A Witch could choose to ask their dead relatives for protection, spiritual blessings, and so on. I shed more light on this later in this section.

The most important lesson for you as a new Wiccan at this point is that irrespective of the deities you believe in, the spiritual beings should be accorded primacy and be invited to be part of your daily life and rituals because, without them, nothing can be achieved. Furthermore, they can be communicated with via several methods, including tarots and runes.

THE DIVINE IS PRESENT IN NATURE

Although Wicca gives priority to the path of spirituality, it does not hesitate to emphasize the value of nature. This belief is not without historical basis. The culture in which Wicca was originally found placed so much value on the environment because it considered natural things to be equally important to life. Furthermore, Wiccans now hold the animistic belief that everything in nature contains the Divine presence. They respect animals, value plants, cherish insects, nurture trees, and engage in such similar acts that affirm the power, influence, and purity of nature.

INITIATION IS VITAL; SELF-INITIATION IS ALLOWED

You must have been wondering how Wicca gets new members. Does it preach to nonmembers with the aim to convert them? Is membership inherited? Does it enforce membership on people? These ideas are very much unlike the nature of Wicca, so you can rightly conclude that the answer to each of them is no! An individual first signifies interest in becoming a Wiccan when they make contact with a Witch or a Wiccan activity. This might be through personal contact as more people now declare their membership, or through the Wiccan public rituals and festivals, or any other possible ways. To become a Wiccan, there are two options available to such persons: study and practice on their own or join a coven. To start with the second option, the seeker will undergo an apprenticeship period of about 12 months and one day, after which, if worthy of initiation after series of studies, would then be initiated into the coven. Some covens call the apprenticeship period the first initiation and after the period of a year, the seeker is then fully initiated. Whichever way it is called, no nonmember is fully initiated just by signifying an interest. They must show themselves to be worthy. The second or real initiation involves a fair ceremony in the sacred circle. Men are initiated by the High Priestess while women are initiated by the High Priest. An initiate becomes a member of the first degree but can progress through the ranks over time if they study well enough for it. Each of the degrees has its corresponding ritual. The sexual ritual occurs at the third degree. But then, what happens if a seeker does not wish to join a coven. Self-initiation is the answer. As Wicca is essentially individualistic, it gives room for self-initiation. This would as well require a detailed study and a personal ritual, which may involve a ritual bath, anointing, and the likes. A self-initiated Wiccan is recognized in the Wiccan tradition as much as the one initiated in the coven.

THE WHEEL OF THE YEAR IS BASED ON SEASONS

There are quite a number of annual celebrations and festivals in Wicca for both Wiccans and non-Wiccans to participate in. These festivals are called Esbats and Sabbats and are, together, known as *The Wheel of the Year*. They are dependent on elements of nature such as the moon (Esbats) and the seasons of the year such as Autumn, Spring, and the likes. The festivals are often done in public, and they involve feasting and merriments.

MAGIC IS A TOOL FOR SELF-EXPRESSION

Magic holds a central position in Wicca. Although it is not a compulsory practice, it reflects at various stages of the Witch's life and activities. Generally speaking, magick is not the sole property of Wiccans. Literally anyone of any religion who takes the extra work to study and imbibe the skills can do magic. However, Wiccans make to differentiate their practice of magick from the stage entertainment performed by most non-Wiccans. The Wiccan magick involves series of spellwork, candles, incantation, crystals and several other items. The aim is to influence the supernatural realm to cause a change in the physical world. The changes in question are always for positive purposes such as blessings, healing, productivity at work, good luck, protection, warding off negative spirits, and making or keeping friends, among many others. It takes three main forms: magick with candles, magick with crystals and magick with herbs. For Wiccans, magick is always for a good cause.

However, the Wiccan Threefold rule and the Wiccan Rede are ways of guiding members in their use of magick. So, if you are looking to become a Witch because you want to mete out punishment on someone who has offended you or you want to bring ill luck to a colleague at work, or any other negative reason, you might as well give it up at this point. The Wiccan magick is not for such intents.

THERE IS LIFE AFTER NOW

Wiccans believe in life after now but definitely not in the Christian concept of eternity. While Christians hold that the dead will end ultimately in either heaven or hell, Wiccans are of the belief that existence is an endless cycle in which those who die will reincarnate and come back on earth to spend another lifetime. It is also the belief that as people die, they temporarily stay at a beautiful place called Summerland (more like the Christian understanding of Paradise), where they are cleansed and prepared for a fresh lifetime. Karma is one other dimension that must be mentioned here. Wiccans hold that what one does in a present life will affect the following life. In a way, this also serves as an explanation for the unpleasant things that happen to people. Most times, Wiccans believe that it is the consequence of one's actions in a former life. This is The Law of Threefold Return. Whatever you do now, you will get back three times as much, either in the present life or in the lives to come. This is why the Wiccan Rede is emphasized: harm no one. The only hitch with the Wiccan theory about the afterlife is that there seems to be no temporal target. Even the Summerland, for all of its beauty, is not the ultimate aim. Souls will still have to return to earth after spending some time there. Does the cycle ever end? There is no end to the dimensions from which Wiccan beliefs can be studied. This is due to the fact that so many innumerable covens and traditions have grown over time with their respective imprints and preferences. As a result, it is a herculean task to compile a thoroughly comprehensive list of beliefs and guide principles that form the foundations in Wicca. Notwithstanding, there are several areas of similitude of beliefs, some of which are the elevation of nature, acceptance of the Wiccan Reed and the annual Wheel of the Year.

WHAT DOES IT MEAN TO BE A WICCAN?

As you proceed in the journey of understanding your Wiccan path, you must bear in mind that it is a steady journey over the course of which you will make lots of personal discoveries. In addition to the foundational truths you have learned in the first section of this chapter, you necessarily have to poise yourself for more and deeper meanings lurking on the path. What I intend to do in this chapter is to prepare you for this discovery. It is expedient to know what is expected of you as a Wiccan, what being a Wiccan implies and requires of you, as well as what you need to do to make the best of this spiritual path.

A WICCAN IS A READER

Perhaps this is the most basic responsibility expected of you as a new or potential witch. I don't mean to scare you, but if you have an aversion to extensive reading, you might have some difficulty getting far in Wicca. To start with, for you to get initiated into the religion, you need to undergo an apprenticeship period of 366 to 367 days, which practically involves reading and extensive study of the Wiccan principles, beliefs, rituals, basic spells, crystals, and other associated elements. The outcome of this period of study will determine whether or not you will get initiated into a coven. After scaling this stage, you will also need to study and practice to go further up the ladder. Books on different topics in Wicca are available in various forms for your preference. Now you wonder why a religion involves so much reading? The answer is not farfetched. Wicca is not dogmatic and is, in all ways, individualistic. What this means is that rather than feed you with all the information you would need to start up your Wiccan journey, you are encouraged to study and discover the realities yourself and understand them your own way. This leads to the next point.

A WICCAN IS A THINKER

Wicca is a modern religion with very little room for dogmatic teachings, but places great emphasis on personal critical reasoning. It is, after all, a product of a modern man's proactive reasoning, Gerald Gardener, who foresaw what would become of the ancient Wicca. In Wicca, it is not enough to read, you must think actively as well. During the apprenticeship period, you are expected to logically and scientifically interact with the Wiccan books you encounter. Do not forget that the books are products of some other Wiccans' reasoning. You are entitled to yours too. It is expected of you to constructively challenge existing norms, query the practices, and question the beliefs, not with a view to demeaning or destroying them, but to personally interact with them to see which ones apply to you and which ones are not suitable. This explains why you can find no Holy Book or a set of commandments in Wicca. More so, it accounts for the increasing diversification. People are created in unique ways. Why should their system of worship be the same? As a thinker, the foundational idea is for you to identify what works for you and what does not.

A WICCAN PRAYS

I have so much emphasized rationality and individuality so far, but lest you forget that Wicca is a spiritual path, bear in mind that praying is a major duty expected of you as a new or potential Wiccan. Mind you, practicing Wiccans are not left out. Praying is a continuous wholehearted activity. In a bid to connect to the deity or deities which you have aligned with, you need to perpetually reach out to them in the spirit realm. Note that it is through prayers that you can make requests of your God and/or Goddess or smaller deities as the case may be. It is during your prayer hours that you get to make your daily demands, which may be for your personal material increase or for spiritual development. In addition, meditation goes hand in hand with prayers. It completes the cycle of communication, so not only do you talk to your deities, but you also have a moment of listening to have your requests, guidance, instructions, etc. confirmed.

Sometimes, Wiccans use items such as burning herbs, crystals and especially candles to facilitate their prayers and meditation. Every Wiccan is prepared to pray. You must be too

A WICCAN IS AN OBSERVER

No, not the passive onlooker! To be a successful Wiccan, and by 'successful' I mean making the best of your spiritual journey, you need to actively engage the Wiccan activities. Bear in mind that growing in Wicca is centered on your ability to learn and practice. Observe the ongoings around you, especially if you are in a coven. Ask questions, make inquiries and find answers. Observe the nature, the seasons, the sun, the moon, the classic elements, the plants around, and on and on. The aim is to help you develop a personal relationship with these elements and apply the knowledge to your everyday life.

A WICCAN IS A BUILDER

Being a Witch involves a gradual process of growth. Growth consists of a variety of activities, one of which is advancing from minor rituals to formal rituals. As a Wiccan, you must be willing to try something new at each point in time. In a slow and steady pattern, you should take on a new ritual, add a new tool, learn a new spellwork, a new invocation, and so on. There is no room for stagnancy in Wicca. To make the best of your Wiccan journey, be ready to grow!

A WICCAN NETWORKS

Does it matter whether you are a solitary Witch or you belong in a coven? The answer is in the negative. Irrespective of your Wiccan orientation, it is a key requirement to connect with other Witches from time to time. There is a place of personal growth, and there is a place for communal affairs as well. Although Wicca emphasizes the individual connection with yourself and the spirit world, it encourages a friendly relationship with other Wiccans as well. As a solitary Witch, you might choose to partly associate with one coven or the other and be part of their public rituals and festivals. Meeting with other Wiccans definitely holds its own benefits. You encounter new persons of the same faith, establish your feet if you have been losing track of the spiritual target, gain new ideas and find people you can contact when you are in one need or the other.

So far in this chapter, I have exposed you to what it means and what it requires to be a Witch. As you would have discovered already, there is no end to what you can be and what you can do in Wicca. It all depends on how far you are willing to go. It is definitely an interesting and expository experience. Once you are convinced about becoming a Witch, be sure to start on the right foot and make the decision to make the best of the journey.

CHAPTER SUMMARY

Have you made the decision to become a Witch? Three is always a starting point. In addition to providing you with helpful tools that will guide you all along, this expository chapter tells you the implications of your being a Wiccan.

CHAPTER THREE.

HOW TO HARNESS YOUR WICCAN MAGIC

RELATIONSHIP BETWEEN MAGIC AND WICCA

More often than not, there is the question asked to know to what extent can the realm of magic and that of Wicca be related. How can these two worlds be related? It is based on this foregoing premise that I write in this section of the book about the ways and procedures to take as a believer in the ways of Wicca to harness your magical potentials. Apart from this, I will also be giving a deep insight into the different worlds of both magic and the religion of Wicca.

In the course of this chapter, I will let you into the different but similar worlds of Wicca and Magic, as I will show how believers in the faith of Wicca deal with the concept of magic and spell casting, as well as reveal the types of magic you can encounter and the tools needed as well to perform these magical procedures and spell casting. I will go ahead also by releasing tips that will help you in your various offerings to utilize your Wiccan magick to the fullest of its potentials. And, for those who have not even detected or have a proper understanding of how much they can do with the power of Wiccan magic they possess.

These two worlds or if you will, aspects in the world of religions and worship are in different ways elements in a concurrent space as well as they are not entirely similar in all their attributes, practices, beliefs, value system and their ways of living in general. The practice in the world of magic has quite evolved over time and has now reached a state of refinement. This is the same in the case of Wicca as a religion.

There have been several notable persons who have influenced the development of these different parts in the world of religions, spirituality and mysticism in general through their works of research, study, spiritual dedication and what have you. In the same light, when we set aside these all mentioned earlier, there have been controversies over the place of magic in the space of the religion, Wicca. Questions abound about the reception of magic in the world of Wicca as a religion and the central place of magic in the worship of Wiccans as religious adherents. Whether magic is an exclusive feature of Wicca is also one of the questions to consider when working on the relationship between these two worlds of wide differences and yet hermetic relationship.

There are a lot of different views scattered all around amongst Wiccans on what magic is. Many Wiccans hold a different belief that sees magic as being an implementation of the dictates invoked through the procedures and practices of witchcraft as well as that of sorcery simply for the purpose of manipulation. These Wiccans are of the opinion that to use magic one must first have had sufficient proficiency in the dealings and workings of witchcraft or sorcery or sometimes both, as the case may be. In short, this set of Wiccans holds a belief that sees magic as a product of both witchcraft and sorcery and also believes that it has a manipulative purpose.

Other Wiccans also, on the other hand, hold the view of certain ceremonial magicians on the meaning of magic. These ceremonial magicians define magic in certain ways, and each of their definitions reveals a new aspect of magic. One such definition given by these ceremonial magicians is that of Aleister Crowley, who offered the definition that magic is "the science and art of causing change in conformity with the will." This definition still considers magic in conformity with the motive of manipulation. Another definition was given by another ceremonial magician who happened to be very prominent at the time. The definition is that of MacGregor Mathers. He defined magic as 'the science of the control of the secret forces of nature'. With this definition, he reveals the workings of magic as a reflection of an order given to certain forces that in the space of nature but are nevertheless kept secret, by someone who has acquired mastery of what he termed as "the science of control....".

The view of MacGregor Mathers reflects what a lot of Wiccans believe in. These Wiccans believe that the workings of magic have nothing to do with the supernatural world at all. This set of Wiccans only holds the belief that these works of magic are only elements that simply agree to the laws that nature as a whole but have not yet been regarded as works that are in concordance with the norms of science judging by the standards of the field of contemporary science. They do not accept the belief that any of the workings of magic are in any way related to the realm of the spiritual, but rather that all of the procedures and practices of magic are a part in the realm of the natural where certain superpowers reside. These parts are what were referred to as the "superpowers that reside in the natural" by another prominent Wiccan known as Leo Martello. Some Wiccans, for their part, see magic as the practical use of only the five senses given to humans, while others see magic as what has worked, since they do not assume in any respect that they know how magic works. They simply just accept that it is true simply because it has been done right there in their presence. This set of Wiccans lay no claim to having a knowledge of how it works in the realm of magic and make no secret of their ignorance. They simply ride along with the experiential effects (magical displays that have been revealed to them).

Wiccans also hold ritual practices where they cast spells to bring out the experiential of their wills in real life. These rituals are always conducted in their sacred circle. They use their magical spells and workings for different purposes, which may be for the following reasons:

First, they conduct their magical rituals for the sake of healing. Some of them also do this in order to get rid of the influences that have been deemed adverse. Some other Wiccans, on the other hand, use their spells and magical works for the spiritual benefits of their personal protection as individuals in the real world. These magical spells can also be used for the sake of boosting fertility.

These are only a few of the numerous purposes magical spells and workings can serve among Wiccans. There are several other benefits to gain from the use of magic as a believer in the faith of the Wiccans. The belief in magical workings and spell works is not peculiar to a section of the Wiccans, as it is a general norm amongst the entirety of believers in the religion known as Wicca.

In general, Wiccans see magic as a manipulative influence on the natural by similar yet hidden parts of nature, which is just for them a set of aptitude or knack as the case may be. There is simply no supernaturality in the working of magic. Such is the belief held universally within Wicca about magic and the workings of this craft. Wiccans view magic simply as just perfecting your natural abilities, and, having harnessed such abilities, focusing them on workings and activities that will, in turn, have real-life effects on the natural world around them in which they live-in. For them, magic is simply a dexterous act. They even make use of certain instruments for this act of 'spellcraft' or, if you like, magic. They make use of the following instruments whenever they want to perform their 'spell works' or magic:

- Athame

- Candles

- Wands

- Incense

- Magical Oils

- Tarot Cards

- Herbs

- Crystals

- Sacred Circle.

These are the different tools necessary to perform magic, especially amongst Wiccans.

However, it will be expedient to note that within Wicca, the ability to conduct 'spell works' or magic is not exclusively given to those that are priests. This is true, as anyone can go on to competently and singlehandedly work magical works without necessarily needing to undergo any rigorous practice or training at all. A little bit of practice will do for whoever wishes to perform magic amongst Wiccans.

Another thing worthy of mention is the singular fact that unlike what is obtainable in other kinds of religions, most especially other magical religions, where there are some stipulations like a universal code of conduct that has been set aside to take effect on the dealings of magic and casting of spells, there is nothing of such as regards the dealings concerning magic within Wicca. There is no framework or precept, either conventional or statutory, that serves as a guide for deducing the manner or method in which magical workings should be performed. However, some Wiccans have adopted certain codes to guide their own magical acts. The "Law of the Triple Return" or "The Rule of Three" is what guides some Wiccans, as they have chosen to conform to these statutory codes by choice and will. While, on the other hand, others may decide to strictly adhere to another code that guides the magical procedures that are known as 'La Rede Wicca'. None of these aforementioned codes exists as a universal code of conduct or guideline that guides the workings of magic and its procedures. None of them are universal, adherence to any of these codes is based on the discretion of any Wiccan, except in cases where a Wiccan belongs to a certain group that holds any of these codes as statutory. However, where this is not the case, it is not mandatory. To sum it all up, the workings of magic are not peculiar to any of the religions. It is not a component of Buddhism, Curanderos amongst the Latinos in the Latin America and its healing as well as it is not also a component of Heka and its magical practices amongst the Egyptians or the fetish charms found amongst the Appalachians or even within the Wiccans were it began as a procedure to perform the healing works done by the folk healers that lived centuries ago in the European part of the world. Even having known this, magical works still abound as an evolving art amongst the Wiccans as new techniques and strategies are being developed over time as it has been conceived amongst the Wiccans to just be an exercise of natural energies as well as dexterities that have been properly harnessed and are now used to cause experiential effects in the physical world around them as human beings.

WHAT ARE THE TYPES OF WICCAN MAGIC?

There are different shades of magic and casting of spells as it is being used in the world of religion, which is also known as Wiccan.

As the procedures transcend from divinations to dances, then to the processes that more of the charms and other materials used for these magical ritual purposes (the hands-on workings procedures), many proceedings are revealed. However, certain types are peculiar in their own procedures and they also are quite popular amongst most Wiccans (both witches from ages past and those that are referred to as the modern witches). These types are the ones that are going to be mentioned and briefly explained for the purpose of this chapter.

We have varieties of magic that exist in the religion, Wicca. They are based on the elements they harness in order to work their different magical works. Amongst these types of magic, we have the following that will be briefly explained as follows:

Crystal Magic: This is one of the very prominent types of magic that have been widely accepted within Wicca. This type of magic is developed on the powers or if you want to call it the natural energy of the crystal element. Wiccans view the element referred to as crystal as a living element with a pure energy. The crystal is believed to be an element that gives the energy to effect healing to humans, animals and even plants alike. Crystal, like other natural phenomena, is believed to carry certain energies that can be used for healing purposes. And also, like other natural minerals and stones, a flowing river, as well as other natural elements such as wind, crystal is believed to be another type of energy that, if harnessed properly, can be sent out into the natural world itself to serve specific purposes.

Candle Magic: Here, the element beckoned upon to satisfy the yearnings of the Wiccans as regards magical procedures and casting of spells is the candle. This has been chosen by several Wiccans as the most advisable level for any beginner in the line of Wiccan magic to take-off from. This is due to its appealing state and the basic and straightforwardness of this kind of magic. The beauty of this magic arises from the flamboyant use of different candle colors. The procedures see a candle that burns out from the physical into a different realm of the spirit to which it will carry along all of the intentions and thoughts that have been passed through it as a magical medium. The manifestation of this spirituality is done and witnessed directly in the physical world, and this will aid the understanding of the process. This feature of this kind of magic provides for simplicity and makes it easier to understand how the process went, especially to the good of beginners' understanding in the Wiccan magic.

Herbal Magic: Herbal magic has over time been accepted as the most practical as well as realistic kind of magic as it seeks to explore the potency of simple materials that we can see around us. Some of which are materials we use from day to day. Over time, this has appeared to be the most conforming kind of magic to the norm of magic as this kind of magic more often than not employs the use of the most basic of ingredients for magical rituals, which are herbs. Even when it comes to discussions concerning hands-on magic, herbs come forth as the most relevant and efficient element or ingredients for such magical procedures. These different kinds of magic are dependent on certain elements that are natural and these natural elements transmit certain energies upon which the different kinds of magical rituals are harnessed and directed towards certain effects in the physical world around.

IMPORTANT PRINCIPLES TO NOTE IN ORDER TO HARNESS YOUR WICCAN MAGIC

This is, in fact, the main part of this entire chapter, as it gives an exposition on the steps to take as well as the guidelines to follow if you really want to harness your Wiccan magical powers.

For some people, the whole discussion concerning the dimensions and the different views of different people of their psychic power or, more directly, their Wiccan power of magic is a different ball game altogether. From the person who has noticed their intrinsic powers of divination, wit and others, to the other who has kept their own power(s) latent within them and the one who has no knowledge of what it means to have any power at all.

No matter what your situation as a person currently is, there are certain steps you must take to ignite your magical powers and help you harness them from level to level until they reach their full potential. These processes are gradual and will help your various Wiccan magical powers progress and transcend to a full-fledged one with the potentials properly harnessed and developed.

First of all, you have to find a way to seclude a part of your room that will be for you a sacred place anywhere in your house. However, it is mandatory that the place you have decided to choose as your sacred place be in a place where you will never be disturbed by any person, any noise or any form of distraction, just as this place you have chosen as your "sacred place" must be where you can find freedom to work well on your practice. Apart from that, you must adorn it with pendants, jewels, crystals, amulets or talisman. In general, you need a safe, comfortable and quiet place for your practice.

Another important nugget for harnessing your Wiccan magical powers is your ability to know the different elements, i.e., their representation and meaning(s).

So too, you must cultivate the ability for meditation. This is how this act encourages you to open your mind and helps you key in on the potentials of your harnessed Wiccan magical powers.

You should also undergo the process called the silver light meditation. At this point, you meditate in the environment of candles lit up, incense as well as an oil burner. With all of these, sit comfortably and have your back straight. Also, stay flat-footed on the ground and place your palms on your knees with them facing up. But if you are seated, stretch your legs forward and ace your hands in a similar position on your legs.

Do the following also to properly harness your Wiccan magical powers:

- Breath in and exhale slowly with your eyes closed.

- Visualize a sparkling light of the color kind of silvery-white rising through the spine up to your head and pouring forth from your head.

- Empty your thoughts, get rid of movements and breathe rhythmically. Stay Still!

- Do also the candle meditation and the chakra meditation. The chakras will help you in the meditation process.

- Get aware of your intuition by thinking outside your five senses.

There are also some terms to take note of from Clairaudience to channeling and automatic writing, clairvoyance, and several others. Knowledge of all this will help you to harness your Wiccan magical powers properly without any problems.

CHAPTER SUMMARY

Is Wicca magic? Is magic compulsory in Wicca? Are all Wiccans magicians? What do I need to practice magic as a Witch? I'm quite sure you have many more questions on your mind. Find answers to all your questions about the relationship between magic and Wicca in this chapter.

CHAPTER FOUR.

UNDERSTANDING HERBAL MAGIC

THE CRAFT OF SELECTING HERBS FOR WICCAN RITUALS AND MAGICK

Herbs were originally used for medicinal purposes. But as humans continued to dig deeper into spiritual affairs and the associated activities, they began to realize the supernatural and magical properties of plants and herbs. The initial practice was to use herbs for healing and accompany it with simple words of prayers for effectiveness. Today, herbal magic makes up one of the key components of magic and rituals in Wicca. Who would have thought that 'mere' leaves could work wonders in the supernatural realm? That is the reaction when you realize the magical powers that herbs possess. Thanks to the productive, therapeutic, magical and transformative works of nature. It will interest you to learn that herbal magic on its own is a broad aspect in Wicca that deserves a much-detailed exposition on its own. However, because this is a rather introductory guide into the basics of Wicca, I usher you into the foundational use of herbs for magic. It is my belief that after your encounter with this chapter, you will be well-poised to use herbs, plants, leaves, and flowers for diverse purposes of your choice, ranging from protection to meditation to healing to provision and blessings, among others. The functionality of herbs is not without its association with the five elements which serve as the source of energy for life, fertility, and productivity. Earth provides the life needed for buried seeds to grow into plants and establish their roots. Meanwhile, this is not possible if the minerals and water present on the earth are not in place. But that is not all. The fire element is provided in the form of the sun to provide energy for growth, without which no plant can survive. In addition, the Wind element is useful for the pollination of plants, and the fifth element — Spirit — is accountable for the intrinsic ability of these plants to perform the magic required. Together, the five elements work to bring about the efficiency of herbal magic. As a matter of fact, it is the energies deposited into the herbs that Wiccans tap into to bring about their desired change. This is the simple explanation behind herbal magical powers. The technicality, however, lies in understanding the specific magical powers of each seed, flower, root, bark, berry, stem, and so on, as well as the specific regulations guiding how to apply each of them. Before I list out some of the most common herbs used in herbal magic, and their respective features and functions, here are some of the ways you can put herbs to use:

SMUDGING

This is done by burning the herbs. The resultant smoke and smell are believed to be useful for cleansing during rituals or meditation and for warding off evil spirits. Some Witches prefer to use it as an incense. This has been a rather long-term practice of using herbs and flowers.

BATHING

Healing baths often involve the use of herbs. Fresh or dried herbs are tied in small bags that are placed in the bath. In most cases, it is done using a large bath tube in which the beneficiary of the ritual will lie completely immersed.

Incense may follow depending on the coven. The process is started and ended with a series of ritual spells and incantations.

ESSENTIAL OILS

Another important and efficient way people use herbs is in the form of oils. Oils make up a large part of Wiccan activities and rituals especially. Some herbs can be converted into oils.

On the other hand, some are put directly into ready-made oils and left in them for a few days. Some oils can be applied to the skin, but most are used for aromatherapy, that is, strictly for inhalation.

TEAS AND COFFEES

It is a common practice among Wiccans to use herbs for teas and other drinks. Of course, this only works with herbs that are edible since some could be outrightly poisonous. Some herbal drinks are made in bags and can be bought at supermarkets and in beverage stores, while some necessarily have to be homemade. With the required herbs steeped in hot water for some time, you would have your self-made herbal drink.

CHARMS AND SPELLS

Did you know that charms could be made from herbs? Very well, yes! Different charms work for different purposes just by physical contact. All you would need to do is activate it with one or two spells, and you're good to go! Some can be made into bags or other smaller items that can be carried about. Although herbal therapy requires a deep knowledge of the respective herb you wish to use each time, it is definitely a trusted method of magical healing and rituals. It can also be used with crystal therapy and can be embedded in homemade candles or applied to the surface of oiled candles for use in candle magic. In the next part of this chapter, you will find some of the most common herbs used in Wiccan herbalism, their magical properties, as well as some information on how to use them.

ADDER'S TONGUE

Adder's tongue is particularly useful for spells and charms to stop gossip and slander and to promote healing. It is also known as the Serpent's Tongue and is often considered sacred to those gods associated with snakes.

ALLSPICE

Allspice, as the name implies, is a wonderful spice used for success in business and also to relieve mental tension. It promotes determination and energy. It is also used in spells and charms that involve money and luck. More so, it can be used as a healing herb and can be used to create a healing herbal bath.

ANGELICA ROOT

Also known as Holy Ghost root and Archangel root, this root is essentially female and children-oriented. It is good for protecting children from adverse spirits and enhances female strength. It is also useful for purification, for canceling evil spells, healing baths and for removing curses.

MINT

Mint is also related to the female gender. It helps to clear headaches especially. Simply inhale the steam from it while boiling in hot water. It can promote effective communication and energize one. In addition, it is known to bring happiness and good luck to a home.

BAY LEAVES

Bay leaves are light and easy to carry about. They are masculine in orientation, provide strength and can protect you from being jinxed.

You can leave them under your pillow, carry them to work or scatter them on the floor before sweeping in order to protect your household.

BELLADONNA

Belladonna is one of the dangerous herbs you should handle with care because it is highly poisonous. It should never be ingested but can be used with ointments to alter one's mind. It is also used with protection spells. It must be used with extreme care because it has been reported to result in deaths. If you are a new Witch, I would rather recommend that you stay away from Belladonna.

CHAMOMILE

This beautiful herb helps to relieve stress, brings luck and is also used for purification purposes. If you have difficulty sleeping, focusing on your meditation or relaxing, simply sprinkle it around your home. You could also use it to protect against evil or magical attacks.

For gamblers, chamomile brings good luck! You could wear it like a garland around your neck or, if you are not so daring, simply carry some of them in your pocket, and you're good to go!

CACTUS

This herb is specialized in the protection and banishment of evil spirits. It does not require great efforts. Simply plant it around your home, specifically in all the four directions of North, East, South, and West, and it does its job effectively.

LAVENDER

Like chamomile, lavender brings about relief and calmness. But one important purpose people use lavender for is love.

If you have problems with hatred or you suffer too much rejection from people, you need love, and lavender does the magic for you. Carry it around with you everywhere you go or hang it in your home. If you are mentally troubled or you find it difficult to sleep, stuff a few lavender pieces underneath your pillow before going to bed, and you're bound to get a peaceful sleep.

DEER'S TONGUE

The Deer's Tongue deals with the power of speech and communication. It is often used by lawyers, marketers, orators, and lovers when proposing to their partners. It gives you an eloquence and the power to convince others. Simply carry it about.

FIVE FINGER GRASS

This herb is used for a variety of purposes. First, it could bring you luck in terms of finance and love. It also brings favor to gamblers and business people. In addition, it can be used for purification and for removing hexes. Some Witches prefer to call it Cinquefoil or just Five Fingers.

ROSEMARY

One of the known ancient herbs, Rosemary has always been used for promoting love in an atmosphere where it is needed by warding off negative energy.

But beyond that, it also helps to strengthen the human brain, aids reasoning and remembrance, as well as protects from evil spirits.

You can choose to burn it while meditating to keep your arena safe from negative vibes. Modern Wiccans now also use Rosemary to protect their homes from burglars. Simply hang it at your doorpost.

HIGH JOHN

It is a multipurpose herb that is often worn as an amulet. It is very effective in strengthening the sexual prowess of men. It is also used for making oils and can be incorporated into incense and powders. High John gives luck, protection, financial blessings, success, and strength, among others. It is also known as The Conqueror Root.

SAGE

Sage is useful for various magical goals. For generations, people have used sage for purifying their homes and environment and also for cleansing, especially during rituals. This is done by burning dry sage twigs. However, it has been adopted for more uses than that. Inhaling the smoke is believed to sharpen one's mind and increase one's wisdom. In addition, sage could bring your wishes to reality. This is done by writing your wishes on a sage leaf and leaving the leaf under your pillow. It is believed that if you dream of your wish within the next three to five days, your wish will come to pass.

JASMINE

Jasmine is essentially used as charms for inviting wealth and other forms of blessings. It helps to get a clear mind, gives inspiration and provides working ideas. To apply, burn it as an incense in your bedroom or simply place it under your pillow.

MUGWORT

Mugwort is a trusted herb for increasing productivity and also for mental abilities. It is highly versatile, can be grown in any environment. It can also be used in diverse situations, ranging from smudging to spellwork to incense. If you would like to use mugwort to bring productivity at your workplace of fertility in your home, all you have to do is burn it in the arena or smudge it during divination rituals. Mugwort is, however, forbidden to be touched by pregnant women.

FENNEL SEED

Fennel seed is especially good for protection, courage development and purification. For people who are possessed by one adverse spirit or the other, fennel seeds help to liberate them. Medicinally, it is useful for cooking, helps to reduce weight and aids digestion.

LEMONGRASS

You must have probably seen or heard of lemongrass. It is useful for various purposes ranging from medicinal to magical. It helps to fight indigestion, nausea, and insomnia when taken in the form of tea. It also clears the vital inner organs such as the kidney and the bladder and can help to remove excess body fat. More so, it helps you to relax easily, eradicates tension and aches. When planted in the garden, lemongrass keeps mosquitoes away.

YARROW

If you often lose courage or develop heavy feet when it is time to make valid decisions or take important steps, you definitely lack courage, and this is the right herb for you. All you need to do is to wear it on you when you need the confidence to carry out something important. It magically subdues your low self-esteem, overcomes your fears and boosts your confidence level. Also known as Knight's Milfoil or Woundwort, yarrow is useful for treating injuries too. Some Wiccan groups use it for boosting passionate love in marriage. Simply hang it over your bed!

CINNAMON

Cinnamon is another herb primarily for men. It focuses on increasing a man's strength and sexual ability. It can also be used for love spells, increasing spirituality and enhancing prosperity. Most people, even non-Wiccans, use cinnamon as a spice for food.

Other common herbs that are predominantly used in Wicca are Dandelion, Basil, Hibiscus, Star Anise, Thyme, Nutmeg, Elecampane, Valerian, fern leaf, frankincense, Devil Pod, Epsom salt, Daisy, Daffodils, coltsfoot, and chives among a host of others. While herbs are best gotten when they are fresh, it is not advisable to plan every herb you need. You can procure them from dealers of herbs or from online stores. Like I mentioned earlier, the information about herbs could be teeming. As a matter of fact, the list provided here is simply a fraction of the available plants and herbs used in herbal magic. The list is endless! The point of caution for you is not to allow yourself to be carried away with learning all these herbs and their uses. No, you should rather focus on one herb at a time, depending on which one is useful at each point in time. More so, be careful to avoid misuse. Remember that not all of them are ingestible, and some could be highly toxic and dangerous.

CHAPTER SUMMARY

Herbal magic has worked wonders for ages. You can plug into the art too, and enjoy its amazing magical abilities. Learn how to apply herbs for magic here.

CHAPTER FIVE.

AN EXPOSITION TO CANDLE MAGIC

Practically every Witch believes in the power of candle magick and uses it to bring their wishes or intentions to life. The reasons behind this are not so difficult to guess: candles are cheap to procure, and candle magic is extremely effective and less demanding. Very few tools are needed to set up a working candle magic. This is one of the most attractive points of this type of magic, which has enamored many, both Wiccans and non-Wiccans, over the years. One important thing that surprises its users is how candle magic manages to work its wonders despite its simplicity. The answer lies in its nature. You will be interested to know that candle magic is not based on the wax and wick, but on the flame itself. This buttresses the significance of fire as the most basic element required to bring desires to life. Notwithstanding, the melting away of the candle plays its role in the magical process too. Tracing it back to the beginning, the fire has always been an important element in the life and existence of humans for several reasons. Apart from being a physical source of illumination at night and in dark places, it is also used for cooking. In addition, candles are attached to birthday cakes for making wishes. I bet you never knew the foundation of that tradition. This transformative ability of fire is what Witches and non-Wiccans who believe in the power of fire capitalize on for rituals, magic, and wishes. However, it is not true that candle magick rests solely on the fire element for fulfillment. It is rather an alchemy of the five elements that bring about the success of a candle magick. To start with, the flames represent the fire element; the oxygen needed for combustion to occur is symbolic of the Air element; the melting down of the wax represents the liquid state of the Water element; the base on which the candle stands for the Earth element and the spiritual presence needed to transmute the wishes into the spirit realm is symbolic of the Spirit element. It is, therefore, no surprise that although it appears simple, candle magic embodies the entire universal elements.

THE CANDLE COLOR CHARTS AND THEIR SIGNIFICANCE

With so much emphasis on fire, you would be mistaken to think that the candle wax is completely useless in the candle magick. Far from it! If this was so, why not just use flames from any other source, why necessarily candle? This establishes that the candle performs its own functions in the craft. First, the fact that the candle has the ability to melt upon contact with fire and assume semi-liquid and gaseous states is very significant. More so, they come in various colors, which are also instrumental for achieving diverse purposes. Remember that colors have their respective meanings and associations. Candle magic draws on this for fulfillment as well. As a new or potential Witch, a selection of colors to match your desires might be somewhat tasking. Hence, I have provided a comprehensive list of the candle colors as well as what magic purposes they can be used for.

- White: purification, clarity, truth

- Black: banishing negativity, protection, binding, trances

- Red: passion, love, lust, courage, strength, life force

- Pink: friendship, self-love, compassion, empathy, emotional healing, the feminine

- Yellow: joy, energy, creativity, intelligence

- Orange: success, power, encouragement, confidence, authority

- Green: money, luck, fertility, abundance, growth, wealth, prosperity

- Dark blue: depression, vulnerability, changes

- Light blue: health, patience, healing, peace, serenity, meditation

- Purple: psychic powers, wisdom, intuition, hidden knowledge, spiritual power

- Brown: earth or animal-related, grounding, stability, balance

- Silver: reflection, channeling, neutrality

- Gold: attraction, financial gain, victory, authority

Admittedly, some colors could be unavailable or sometimes difficult to get. In cases like this, you could use a white candle. It is universal in purpose. More so, there are various kinds of candles that may be used for candle magic depending on availability. The most common ones are the table candles, followed by taper candles and pillar candles. Others include votive candles, vigil candles, chime candles, figurine candles, birthday candles, seven knob candles, and tea lights. Your candle color and type selection should be based on your goal. You may also combine candles with crystals and herbs, especially if you intend to do an elaborate ritual. The aim of this is to harmonize the powers of spells, stones, and herbs to bring about a speedy fulfillment of the intentions. It is often used in coven rituals, but for very simple personal magic, your candle alone is enough to do the job.

A STEP-BY-STEP GUIDE TO CANDLE MAGICK

Starting up a candle magick is not in any way difficult. After having selected your candle based on the intentions you have in mind, activating the magic is the next step to take. But before you commence the process, you need to cleanse your candle. It is not spiritually healthy to procure a candle and start using it straight away. Candles are capable of receiving vibrations, which may sometimes be negative and detrimental to your goal. To be safe, whether you have just bought the candle or it has been in your custody for some time, be sure to cleanse it before use. The most common way of cleansing candles is by smudging them using a smudge spray or a smudge stick. Incense smoke is also recommendable.

After cleansing your candle, you should bless or charge it. Always bear in mind that a candle is just what it is — a candle — except it is spiritually charged. To get the best of your candle magic, you should charge your candle by saying a word of prayer or related incantation onto it. You might also choose to breathe your intentions into the candle. To do this, simply fill your mind with thoughts of what you want the candle magic to accomplish for you, and then breathe into the candle. Visualize your breath going out of you and into it. A third and likewise simple method is by physically placing your hands over the candle. This way, you are trying to release your energy into it. Upon successfully charging your candle, the next step is to inscribe it. Again, there are a couple of ways to this. For large rituals, inscribing physical intentions or symbols on the candle and thereafter rubbing it .with oil and herbs is the order of the day, but for a solitary Wiccan, that might be too much of a ceremony. You could simply write your wishes on a small folded piece of paper and put it beside the wick to burn during the process.

Having fully prepared the stage and your tools are ready, you should take note of the following simple tips as you select and apply your candle magic:

- Abstain from using the same candle twice. This is because candles are capable of receiving vibrations and could elicit negative results as a result. Use small candles that can burn out in minutes for short magic periods. For rituals, use longer candles.

- Special candles such as short taper candles or votive candles are highly recommendable.

- Accompany your candle magic with short incantations or mantras declaring your desires into reality. You could choose to repeat this silently as you gaze at the candle.

- Inscribe your intentions on the candle or write them on a small piece of paper, fold it carefully and place it in the container to burn.

- Your mental focus should be on your intentions and your physical gaze should be on the burning flames.

- Dispose of the candle wax after the process.

- If you wish to read answers to your requests immediately, simply drop the wax into a bowl of water. It will instantly solidify into shapes. The shapes will form the answers you seek.

- Release the elements after your magic and you have received a conviction that it has come to fulfillment.

It is normal to get excited on your first attempt at any type of magic, and the same can be said of candle magick. As a new Witch, it is highly advisable that you take it one step at a time. Of course, candle magick is the easiest of all magic types, but could sometimes require a few processes. However, as I have already indicated, you do not have to go through the rigors of color selection at your first attempt, especially if you are not sure which color to use for which purpose or the colors are not readily available to you. Use a white candle, focus on your intentions and watch how they manifest into reality.

CHAPTER SUMMARY

The third and arguably the easiest of the three most common magic types is candle magic. Cheap, efficient and easy to use, you will find candle magic a handy tool in your Wiccan journey. Find out all you need to know about it in this chapter.

CHAPTER SIX.

HOW TO SET UP YOUR PERSONAL WICCAN ALTAR

To be altarless is to be voiceless

Steven Chuks Nwaokeke

S teven Chuks could not have put it any better. In virtually every religion, the altar occupies a central position of spiritual activities. For Wicca, the emphasis is even more because the altar serves as the point of bringing to reality all your desires, communing with the Spirit realm, hearing from the deities, performing rituals, and several other religious acts. It can be said with a fair measure of confidence that virtually nothing can be achieved in Wicca without an altar. This buttresses the significance it holds for you even as a potential or new Witch. Altars could be raised in public and private spheres and for different purposes. However, my concern here is centered on helping you raise your personal altar. Raising an altar is not in any way difficult or financially demanding in as much you have the right guides and the proper hacks. So, as I suggest items for your altar in this chapter, I also recommend the low-budget alternatives which can serve the same purpose.

WHAT IS A WICCAN ALTAR?

Put most simply, the Wiccan altar is a raised platform charged with spiritual energies where the Witch performs their rituals, meditation, magick, and other supernatural activities. You would be mistaken to consider the altar a mere physical platform because each of the items put in place to make up a working Wiccan altar holds high spiritual significance and contains the presence of the elements and the deities, which all work together to bring success and fulfillment in whatever activities the Witch engages in.

SETTING UP YOUR PERSONAL ALTAR

An important point to bear in mind before we delve into the steps involved in setting up a working personal altar is that your altar should naturally reflect your personality. What's the implication of this? Notwithstanding the steps provided here, you are the major determinant factor of what goes on your altar and what does not. This is why I have left off discussing the altar till this point when you have expectedly been grounded in the fundamentals of Wicca, and you have made vital decisions for yourself such as whether you want to be duotheistic or monotheistic, a solitary Witch or you want to belong in a coven, and other decisions such as the smaller deities to believe in. Each of these decisions that you have made for yourself will determine how you want your altar to be. Having established that, you must also bear in mind that you need not stuff your altar with all the tools you choose at a time. Before an item goes on your altar, ensure you understand its use and significance and that you have a need for it. Provided below are the most basic rules to guide you:

SELECT YOUR ALTAR SURFACE

This is often a consecrated place on which you place your tools. Any platform whatsoever will serve. It could be a table, a mat, desk, stump or any other similar spot that suits you. Once you have decided that, you should cover it with an altar cloth, which is any piece of cloth meant to serve both as an ornament and for protection of the altar surface. Special altar clothes are sold at Wiccan stores, but you could use any domestic piece of cloth. Ensure you cleanse it.

INDOOR OR OUTDOOR?

Where do you want your altar to be situated? You should also decide which location works best for you. For personal altars, the recommendation is always indoors, not because being outdoors will affect the outcome of your activities, but simply as a measure of focus. You need to situate your altar in an environment where you will be completely free of distractions.

SELECT YOUR TOOLS

This is the point where your religious tools come on the altar. Symbols of your deities should be positioned on the altar. After this, you should decorate it with the basic tools required of every altar. These include symbols of the Goddess or God or both, a cauldron, a chalice, a wand, an athame, the pentacle, candles, censer, a broom, and an incense. Note that these items do not necessarily have to be present all at a time. As a matter of fact, some of them might be difficult to procure depending on your locale. If you cannot find them or you can't afford them, you might want to use the low-budget alternatives, which I provide below. More so, to make you feel at ease, it is advisable to include items such as pictures of nature or loved ones, flowers, and other such items that you love. The fundamental classic tools include the following:

THE PENTACLE

The pentacle is a talisman with the shape of a five-pointed star. It is a representation of the five elements, which are in turn related to the directions of the North, East, South, and West. The fifth point is the ethereal element, the Spirit, which is not bound by space or geography. If you cannot get a standard image of the pentacle, simply have it carved from paper or you draw it on a piece of paper, and you are good to go!

THE CAULDRON

Cauldrons are often earthen vessels designed for cooking in open places. They are used in Wicca for burning herbs, incenses or flowers during meditation. In some cases, they are used to mix and pound ingredients for rituals.

Cauldrons are not so difficult to get, but if you can't find or afford one, any domestic pot will fill the gap.

Your cauldron does not necessarily have to be big, especially for solitary practitioners. A moderate size is enough.

ATHAME

This is a typical knife with a wooden handle. In Wicca, it often comes with a black handle and is used for inscription, drawing circles, casting spells, and warding off negative spirits, among other uses.

There is really no need to buy a new knife for setting up your altar. Any knife will serve this purpose, but be sure not to use it for any other purpose after converting it to your athame.

CHALICE

The chalice is a drinking vessel often used for ceremonial and magical purposes. It is often filled with ashes, herbs, and flowers for spells, rituals, and magic. Again, any cup will serve. Since it performs very similar functions as the cauldron, some Witches prefer to use the same vessel for both. Whatever rocks your boat!

THE WAND

Wands are essential for directing energy and casting spells and rituals. It is often made of sturdy wood so it can withstand the test of time. Wands are readily available in online magic stores. You could also make one for yourself with any wood around.

Other classic elements are the censer, brooms, candles and, of course, incense, as well as the symbols of each of the five elements. In addition to the classic items, you might want to include any of the following decorative items as they suit you;

- Minerals, Crystals, and Rocks

- Live Plants

- Dried Herbs

- Flowers

- Plants

- Jewelry

- Drawings and Crafts

- A bowl of water

On a final note, you must bear these basic rules in mind as you set up your altar: first, your altar is exclusively yours. Before you add anything to it, check whether it suits your interest and personality, and ask yourself whether you have a need for it. Secondly, remember not to clutter your altar with excessive tools.

If you do not need an optional tool for a long period of time, it is advisable to keep it off your altar.

CHAPTER SUMMARY

What is a Witch without an altar? Powerless! Your altar is as important as your rituals and every other Wiccan practice that you have learned so far. To kick-start your Wiccan journey, you need to raise an altar — your altar. This chapter reveals all you need to know about creating your personal altar.

CONCLUSION

4 STEPS TO BECOMING A BETTER WICCAN

There is only one way to do this. Practice, practice, practice!

Donald Michael Kraig

The journey of Wiccans into spiritual fulfillment supersedes the bounds of time. If you have made up your mind to become or remain a full-fledged Witch, as I expect that you would have following the discoveries you have encountered in this book, you must bear in mind that you are in for a rewarding journey that knows no end even after the present life. Based on this, in order to make the best of your Wiccan journey, you must be actively involved in the process, with the heart to grow and become better on a daily basis. To refuse to grow is to choose to die. The only way forward is to become a better Witch. Chances are you are wondering why. In the rest of this chapter, I propose four simple, practicable ideas to help you grow on a daily basis.

PRACTICE MORE

Perhaps the most foundational rule to life is doing and doing more. No growth comes with complacency, and that applies even to you as a Witch. It is, therefore, no wonder that for one to go higher in the ranks of Wiccan coven, you have to prove your ability through practice. Although Wicca emphasizes extensive study, it is not enough just to study. You need to practice as well. To get better in rituals, magick, spell casting, meditating, tarot reading, and other Wiccan activities, the only way is to do more.

TRY SOMETHING OUTSIDE YOUR TRADITION

A different way to put this is to explore! Always bear in mind that you are only one of the millions of Wiccans out there with their respective beliefs, opinions, practices, and prejudices.

Outside your domain of practice lies a vast fertile land comprising novel ideas and practices that you might possibly find interesting and helpful to your practice. The only way to find out such ideas is to keep an open mind and explore them. Wicca does not tolerate dogmatism, so you must be willing to accept new ideas, accommodate others with diverse beliefs, and be ready to exchange knowledge where necessary.

Again, this is not to force you to belong in a coven. Even as a solitary Witch, you could exchange ideas with people online or partake in some public rituals and festivals from time to time. You might as well want to explore books belonging to other religions, just to establish your significance as a Witch in the Global religious circle and to widen your horizon of knowledge.

SPEND TIME WITH NATURE

A larger part of Wicca is based on nature. Apart from the fact that it is founded on a cultural belief that elevates nature and its elements, the Wiccan festivals, which form a core part of every Witch's life and activities, are centered around the cycle of nature known as seasons. In other words, the celebrations of Sabbats and Esbats especially are formed around the movement of the Sun and the Moon. Yet, these are just some of the ways in which Wicca relates to nature. To enjoy a productive and fulfilling Wiccan journey, therefore, a deep understanding of nature is essential. More so, spending time with nature has its personal benefit for you both as a human and a Witch. The inner peace that comes from spending enough time in nature is unsurpassed. Moreover, it sediments and deepens the relationship between oneself and the elements of nature, which come in handy during Wiccan activities.

MAKE SMALL DEVOTIONS AND ACTS OF KINDNESS

The very little things that we often ignore matter a lot. Growth involves working on yourself a lot, and this might sometimes mean becoming conscious of the little things that you would otherwise ignore. If you have a small deity, make little acts of worship to it from time to time. Honor it, show it some appreciation, write Thank You notes, among other little things. Speak with the elements freely as if they were present with you. Appreciate them for being there. Give thanks for the water, the air, the earth and fire in the form of the sun for their contributions to everyday living. You might also want to clean the environment, praise nature or just sit and appreciate it. In the long run, these acts do not only register you as a favorite of the deities, but gives you a feeling of inner peace with yourself and make you a better Witch. If you have patiently and dutifully made it with me to this point, I say congratulations to you. It is my belief that from your journey through this book, you would have made personal discoveries for yourself, identified ways to achieve your Wiccan goals and attain the spiritual peak. As you would have realized, Wicca is many things at a time, and the journey has only just started for you. Do not end here. Determine to enquire more, study more, do more and be more!

THE MORE WE DO,

THE MORE WE CAN DO

-- WILLIAM HAZLITT

WICCA BEGINNERS GUIDE

A Wonderful Guide About Wicca, Including Symbols, Instruments, Spells, Rituals, Celebrations and Festivals

Antony Vithale

INTRODUCTION

Wicca is a very peaceful, harmonious and balanced way of thinking and lifestyle that promotes unity with divinity and all that exists. Wicca is to deeply appreciate and marvel at the sight of a sunrise or sunset, the forest under the bright light of the full moon, or an enchanted meadow with the first light of day. It is the morning dew on the petals of a beautiful flower, the gentle caress of a warm breeze on your skin, or the warmest of summer suns on your face. Wicca is the fall of leaves in Autumn and the delicate descent of snowflakes in Winter. Wicca is light, shadow, and everything contained in between. Wicca is the song of birds and many other creatures.

Wicca is being in the presence of Mother Earth and surprising oneself by making humble obeisances. And when we are in the Temple of the Lord and Lady, we are not prone to the arrogance of human technology, for they touch the depths of our souls. To be Wicca - or to be Wiccan - is to be a healer, a teacher, a seeker, a generous giver and a protector of all things. If this path is truly yours, you can walk it with honor, light and integrity. Wicca is a Religion, a belief system and a Way of Life based largely on the recreation (some call it a reconstruction) of pre-Christian Traditions originating primarily from Ireland, Scotland and Wales - though also from many other parts of the World. While much of the information on how our ancestors lived, worshipped and believed has been lost due to the efforts of the medieval church to erase our existence from history, we try and struggle with the best of our resources to recreate or reconstruct those beliefs using the information we have available. With many recent archaeological discoveries, we now have a tremendous basis for our conviction that our belief system can be traced in the history of the World as far back as the Paleolithic Era, when the first acts of worship, towards the Hunter God and the Goddess of Fertility, took place. With the discovery of these cave paintings, which date back 30,000 years, and some even much older, and which perfectly depict a male hunter with horns on his head and a pregnant woman standing in a circle with eleven other people, it can reasonably be assumed that Witchcraft is the oldest religion ever known. These archetypes are clearly recognized by Wiccans as aspects of the Goddess and the God. Wicca pre-dates Christianity by at least 28,000 years older. "Wicca" meaning "Wise" is now for many another way of saying "Witch", which also comes from the word "Knower"; and "Craft" which by the way means "Art". So, "Witchcraft" ("WitchCraft") would then be "The Art of the Wise". Witchcraft in ancient history was well known as "The Art of the Wise" due in part to the fact that those who followed the path were healers, were in tune with the forces of nature, had extensive knowledge of herbs and medicines, gave advice and, as Shamanic leaders, were valuable parts of Villages, Villages and Communities.

They understood that the human race is not superior to nature, nor to the earth or its creatures, but that we are simply one of many parts, revealed and hidden, that combine to form the Whole. As they would say, "We do not own the Earth, we are part of It." These wise people understood that whatever we take or use, we must give back to maintain balance and equilibrium. Clearly modern man, with all his applied knowledge and technology, has forgotten this. Subsequently, we face ecological disasters and eventual extinction due to our hunger for power and a few pieces of gold.Over the past few hundred years, the image of the Warlock has been erroneously associated with evil, hatred and profanity. In my humble opinion, these misconceptions have their origins in a couple of different places.

To begin with, the Medieval Church between the 15th and 18th centuries created thousands of myths to convert millions of followers of the ancient religions to the new way of thinking: that of the Christian Church. By representing the Witch as a diabolical character, and by converting the Ancient Deities into devils and demons, the missionaries were able to attach terror and revulsion to these beliefs, thus accelerating the conversion process. Continuing with the origins of the misconceptions, the flourishing of allopathic medical science was not of any help either, because from then on all the prestige was taken away from the healers, the Wise Men and the Priestesses. And from this also arose the degradation and discrimination of women, as they were little understood physiologically, especially with regard to issues involving the menstrual cycle, pregnancy and lactation.

Unfortunately many of these unfounded fears, stupid beliefs and absurd fears survived the centuries, and to this day exist. This is the main reason why many who follow the Ancient Way have adopted the name "Wiccan Religion" over the real "Witchcraft" to escape the persecution, harassment, and false beliefs associated with the name "Witch" and "Warlock", not to mention the bad publicity we have been given by the press and Hollywood, who have always used us to generate profit.

CHAPTER ONE.

THE WICCAN SYMBOLS AND THEIR IMPLICATIONS FOR YOU

J ust like every other religion, there are symbols that hold different meanings and significations in Wicca. During the early years, before writing came into place, symbols were the signs of communication. Just as we still have the doing today, especially as road signs, they could inform you of possible danger, direction to turn, a nearby hospital, a sharp turn, or what have you. However, symbols today have gone beyond mere passing information. Especially in religion, they are very significant and they can be used for various important reasons. In this chapter, I will be explaining some of the popular Wiccan symbols, what they mean, and how they can be useful for you as a Wiccan. There are many symbols, but there are generally two classes. The first class has images that stand for unique talismans in the Wiccan world, while the second class consists of elements that are not particularly images but have great significance as well. Below, you will find a list of the symbols under each class.

1. PENTAGRAM

Yes! You guessed right. It is from the prefix "Penta-" which means five. Pentagram is a very popular symbol. Most people, both Wiccans and non-Wiccans, know the symbol and attach it to witchcraft. Pentagram holds a very important significance, and although no symbol is inferior to another, the Pentagram is one symbol that you definitely cannot do without as a Wiccan. The Pentagram is a star in a circle. Perhaps the most important nuance about the Pentagram is that the start must have five points, and all points must touch the inner part of the circle. No matter how you turn the Pentagram or from what angle you behold it, there are always four points below and a point above. This has its explanation. Basically, the goal of Wicca is to influence or manipulate the physical through the spiritual. This symbol embodies that goal. The four points below represent the four traditional elements. They are water, air, earth, and fire. Really, think about it, there's nothing in the world that is not connected to any of these elements. The one point above, as you may guess, represents the outside of the globe -the divine. The divine has different meanings to different Wiccans. To some, it means spirit, to some, it is a God, to others, it is a group of gods and goddesses. Whatever it means to any Wiccan, the consensus on it is that it is supernatural and has a lot of say on what happens in the physical. That's not all. There is a circle. Across different facets of life, a circle represents wholeness and unity. The circle here is not different. Since the four points standing for the four elements are touching the same circle as the divine, then there is harmony between the five, and this harmony can be used during rituals to provoke a change in the physical, by making it meet a touch of the supernatural. The terrestrial and celestial are to always work together to achieve balance. When such is the aim, this symbol could be very important. Before I move to the next symbol, there are basic misconceptions about the nature and positioning of the pentagram. Some people mistake Pentagram for Pentacle. Let's get things straight. First off, Pentagram and Pentacle do not mean exactly the same thing. One of the common misconceptions is that it is only called a Pentagram when the star is facing down. When the star is facing up, it is a Pentacle. No! That's wrong! You may also hear that when the star is facing down, it holds strong sinister or satanic significance. That's also wrong. The positioning of the star changes in line with what you want to achieve. Truly, Satanists may use a downward-facing star for whatever, it doesn't mean Wiccans who use it with a different aim are unknowingly worshipping Satan. For example, for binding and banishment spells, most witches use the downward-facing star because they believe that way, it possesses the power to get rid of negativity.

Another misconception you may encounter is that a Pentagram is simply a star with five points while a Pentacle is the same star in a circle. As euphonious as this sounds, it is incorrect. The misconception is fueled because when the initial parts of "Pentagram" and the last part of "circle" are chopped, a mixture of the chopped parts will result in "Pentacle". The truth is that a pentagram is a five-pointed star contained in a circle. It doesn't matter what direction it is facing; it is a Pentagram. But what then is a Pentacle? A Pentacle is any magical talisman that has a symbol inscribed on it. A Pentacle could be for any purpose depending on what the Witch wants to achieve. So, from the definition, you can rightly say that among others, the Pentagram is a type of Pentacle. Yes, you are 100% correct! So, just as there is a Pentacle called the "Seal of Solomon", there is another called the "Pentagram", and there are others called different names and doing different things. But this particular Pentacle (the Pentagram) effects unity between the spiritual and physical.

2. THE TRIPLE MOON

Every month, the Moon is always on the move. At the beginning of the month, you find the half-moon trying to break out. It continues until it swings to the next stage. At this stage, there is a full moon. After having the full moon, it gradually reduces until you have a half, almost vanishing moon. The moon repeats this process every month. The process is of high significance in the Wiccan world. The three stages are given a pictorial representation in one image and called the Triple Moon. Beyond the stages, it has a greater significance. It stands for the Triple Goddess. The triple Goddess is the greatest representation of feminine divinity in Wicca. It shows the three stages in the Triple Goddess' life and can also be a representation of the three stages in most females' lives. The stages are The Maiden, The Mother, The Crone. The Maiden: Of these three stages, the first is the stage of growth. It is represented by the growing, waxing moon. The Maiden represents love, purity, and new beginnings. It stands for anything that's starting and expecting to grow. The Mother: This is the central scenario of a woman's life. The symbol is represented by a full moon. It is easy to know what this particular shape represents. Mothers protect and care for their children. They give everything they have so that their children can live better lives. They care for their children. Maybe not all mothers, but at least the good ones, one of which is the Goddess. The representation shows the Goddess as a maternal figure that is capable of guidance and protection. It represents the love the Goddess has for all. The Crone: Immediately following the full moon is a gradually vanishing one. It represents the latter stage of life. In the latter stages of life, people quit trusting in their physical strengths. They now rely heavily on experience and mental strength to achieve things. For human beings, the best way to get somewhere early in the last stage of life is not to run, but to get going early. The best way to dance is not by doing jumps and somersaults, but by making simple, intelligent movements. Overconfidence in strength is gone, things take a different approach. This is the exact stage that the third moon represents. It shows the Triple Goddess at the peak of her magical abilities. You don't need anyone to remind you that old age is a stage of great spiritual (not physical) wisdom and power in Wicca. Therefore, the Crone is a symbol that represents divinity, spiritual wisdom and the banishment of negativity.

3. THE HORNED GOD

The name is enough to give some clue as to what the symbol looks like. The Horned God, when viewed from the perspective of his name, looks like there are two horns on a head. When viewed from the perspective of the Triple Goddess, it looks like a crescent moon is resting on a full one. Whatever the perspective, it cannot have a wrong implication in the mind because the horn shows masculinity while seeing it as a moon shows it as a pair to the Triple Goddess. Although there's no third moon, some Wiccans believe it also represents three stages in a Male's life: Master, Father, Sage. All stages hold the same implications as the Triple Goddess'. Before I proceed to the next symbol, I have to explain more about the relationship between the Triple Goddess and the Horned God.

These two are sometimes referred to as the Lord and Lady of Wicca. They are two sides of the same coin and they always work in Unity. Some Wiccans invoke them as a pair and they see greater results than those who invoke them individually. Together, they oversee the universe, and they can influence anything happening on earth.

4. TRIQUETRA

It is also called the Celtic Knot. From the word "knot", you must be guessing the symbol will have a complex confluence at some point. Well, maybe the confluence isn't the reason for the name, but you didn't guess wrong. The rescue of a Triquetra is an image of three leaf-like shapes joining together at the base. This may also be contained in a circle as the Pentagram. In that case, does the description make the Celtic knot a pentacle as explained above? Yes! But what kind of Pentacle would it be? As already said, a circle shows unity and bond. That is retained here. But added to it is that the circle has neither a beginning nor an end. Since its end is not known, it stands for infinity. But contained in it is a bond of three leaf-like shapes that appear to have tips and bases. That's finite. The symbol, therefore, can be interpreted to put some finite lines inside an infinite line for effect. Infinity is an attribute associated with divinity in the Wiccan world. It is also to achieve the goal of magic, which is to influence nature by divinity. Every spell is performed so that the great influence of the supernatural can be clearly felt in the physical in the most perceptible ways to nature and its inhabitants. The Triquetra is a symbol some witches use to represent the Triple Goddess. This isn't entirely wrong because the Goddess is associated with the number three.

5. THE WITCH'S KNOT

The Witch's Knot is a symbol that has lived for centuries. It is very popular among Witches. It can be used to banish or ward off evil. There is an explanation for that. We'll get there. This symbol is a bit different from other symbols. This is because it can be made physical and tangible. While other symbols only have pictorial representations, the Witch's Knot can be made with a rope or twine and held. It looks exactly like four connected semicircles backing each other with little space in between that makes a square. Then a circle drawing over them. In this case, the scribbling is not contained within a circle; rather, the circle is contained within the scribbling. If you have seen this before and you've not treated it with enough respect, there's no cause for alarm, the Witch's Knot is also used in some cases as mere design. The circle within the knot does not only represent infinity, it represents a boundary. Often, in Wicca, when a circle is drawn, it creates a sacred boundary that evil is not powerful enough to get past. It wards off bad energy. That is a very good explanation for why it is seen as a talisman that could be very useful when the spell is to banish or ward off evil. Also striking is the cross-shaped image holding the circle. There is only one consensual interpretation for it: that it has to do with groups of four. Some say it represents the four cardinal points, others say it represents the four traditional elements already mentioned.

Whatever your opinion, you can't go wrong because it performs similar functions in both positions. The four traditional elements are important symbols in Wicca as well. But before I get to that, I'll show you some other important symbols.

6. WHEEL OF THE YEAR

The Wheel of the year may appear in different forms, but that shouldn't confuse you. What is important is it must have eight sections within a circle. After the sections, there could be the triquetra, the pentagram, another circle, or nothing. It remains the wheel of the year. Most of the time, the symbols after the section is just to show that it is related to Wicca.

Therefore, any Wicca symbol can find its way there. The eight sections represent eight major holidays. Other holidays may be celebrated intermittently, as shown on a few Wheel of the Year, but the eight main holidays are what the big sections in the Wheel of the Year stand for. The holidays are Yule (or the Winter Solstice), Imbolc, Ostara (or the Spring Equinox), Beltane, Litha (or the Summer Solstice), Lammas (or Lughnasadh), Mabon (or the Fall Equinox), Samhain. Briefly, let's take a brief look at all eight holidays. Subsequently, in this book, I dedicate a whole chapter to the discussion of the major and minor Wiccan holidays.

Yule/Winter Solstice: It is also called midwinter. Yule represents the beginning or end of the year in the Wiccan world. No wonder it is the first section of the Wheel of the Year. If it falls between December 20 and 23. It is the return of the sun and light. Also, it is the time of the rebirth of the Horned God. It holds an astrological significance as it is the shortest day and longest night of the year. During this time, the celebration takes different forms. Some Wiccans burn the sun candle to show they are welcoming the sun, some ensure they represent the sun in any ritual they make. There are many other ways Wicca is celebrated. Some do by decorating altars with related herbs (like oak, clove, star anise, frankincense, pomegranate, mistletoe, spikenard, myrrh, apple, etc.), and plants (like holly, ivy, evergreen). Whatever way you choose to celebrate yours, ensure there is an actual festival or celebration that day to mark it. Yule is also the best time to cast some spells that involve love, happiness, harmony, etc.

Imbolc: Some people call it Brigid's day. It is a holiday that comes up on either the 1st or 2nd of February. It is a time when the promise of spring is celebrated. Wiccans celebrate the pure joy, emerging life, and growth during this period. During the holiday, some images are common. They include the image of the reunion between the Horned God and the Triple Goddess, an image of crowns of light, etc. The herbs and plants used during this period are bay, iris, coltsfoot, cinnamon, basil, wisteria. Wiccans celebrate Imbolc in different ways. Some light candles and place one in each room in a house, some prepare a feast where they eat, merry, and share a lot, some cast spells to cleanse their energy and prepare for spring, others do some or all of the above.

Ostara: It is also called Spring Equinox. It is a time when the arrival of spring is celebrated. As you can guess, it comes up in March, particularly between the 19th and 22nd. For Wiccans, it is a time of fertility and is represented by imagery featuring the hare and eggs. In Christianity, sometimes, Easter, which comes up around the same period, is also represented with similar imagery. Sometimes, it is also represented by an image of the Sun God and the Maiden Goddess who will become a Mother after nine months. During spring, the days are longer and warmer. Its credit must be given to the sun. It is called Spring Equinox because it is one of the only two days in a year where both night and day are equivalent. It is a time of gratefulness and blessings. It is the right time to set intentions. It is also the time to cast spells of balancing and spring. It is always a bright season filled with joy. Florals like rose and jasmine are the herbs associated with Ostara.

Beltane: It is also called May Day. This holiday, which marks the midpoint between spring and summer, is celebrated from the evening on the 30th of April into the first day in May. During this holiday, various earth energies are released. Some Wiccans see it as the holiday of fire and energy. The last night of May Day is a night with charged sexuality. It is a time when fertility is at its peak. Many years before, Beltane was a time promiscuity was encouraged. Even wedded couples were allowed to "unwed" for the night. In recent years, that has changed. Since Beltane is a feast of fire, whatever way you want to celebrate it, the fire must feature. It could be by taking out all the fire around for a special fire, or some other way. I advise you to look for an open space for a bonfire. It gives you the chance to celebrate it among people who have the knowledge of what you are doing. During this time, you may cast spells that are concerned with unity, fertility, and intimacy. Fire is used for purification, so it is a time for purification.

Litha: It is also called the Summer Solstice. This holiday marks the longest day of the year. It is the official entrance of summer that people have been anticipating since the last holiday. It falls between the 20th and 22nd of June. It is a period when the Sun God is at his strongest. There are light and life all around. Even after work, there's enough light to celebrate.

Most marriages come up during June because it is a time of blessings and abundant joy. Common herbs for this period are honeysuckle, chamomile, mugwort, lemon, wild thyme, and lavender. It is a celebration of the sun. It is a time to give thanks for all you possess. Also, it is the right time to connect to the Earth. You can perform rituals for all these, just make sure you do it in the sun.

Lammas: It is also called Lughnasadh. Not only does this holiday mark the end of summer, but it is also the first of three autumnal harvest festivals. It comes up either on the 31st of July or the 1st of August. It is a time to show gratitude to God and Goddess for seeds and crops. It is a time to be promised a new harvest, as well as increased food. Almost everything is used for celebration during this period. Herbs like sandalwood, heather, and fruits are used. Everything about Lammas is appreciation. It can be easily felt in the air. It is a time everyone is happy for the return of food (which really never left). Some people take it as the time to collect and store seeds and seedlings in preparation for the next spring.

Mabon: It is also called the Fall Equinox. It is the second celebrated harvest, and it occurs between September 21st-23rd. The holiday is the start of autumn and notifies people of the coming dark days. During this time, people are reminded that "we reap what we sow", so people understand that the energy they release into the universe affects a lot. Herbs of this period include marigold, vegetables, sage, and tobacco. Spells of this time are for prosperity, gathering, transformation, and protection. It is also a time to remember people who have died, give offerings to trees and nature generally, as well as request blessings from the Goddess.

Samhain: It is also called Hallow. This is probably the biggest celebration you can find on the Wheel of the Year. It represents the sleep of the Sun God. During this time, the Sun God sleeps off, so do summer and fall, everybody prepares for the approaching winter. The colder months are about to begin, and we would start having longer nights than a day. It comes up on the 31st of October, and it is the third and final harvest festival. Also, this period is a time of remembrance for the loved ones who have waved to this world. The ancestors are celebrated, as well as the balance between life and death. Candles, gourds, black cats, apples are all symbols of the season. The next symbols are categorized as Elemental symbols. They are four and they have been mentioned above. They may not particularly have images that are used to represent them, but they hold a lot of significance and represent quite a lot for them to be seen as symbols. They are earth, fire, water, and air. Although there may be other things in the world, almost everything is rooted in one of these four.

They can all be called nature. Although sometimes, Wiccans invoke a God or Goddess to influence what is happening, most times, Wiccans turn to the power that nature has in itself. The power cannot be underestimated. Although each element has its weakness, whenever all elements are combined in the sacred circle, they become a whole, strong source of power. Find more on each element below.

7. EARTH

In Wicca, the earth is the most pragmatic, practical of all elements. It holds a lot of value. The earth is ancient, therefore, it stands for the wisdom of experience. It has a nature that is constant and unchanging. It has some positive energies in it, which, if released, can help its inhabitants. The earth is a symbol of wisdom. It stands for everything in the present.

8. FIRE

Fire is a symbol of passion, drive, and intensity. Ever heard people saying, "keep the fire going!" Or "fire on!"? Fire is like fuel for humans. During spells, one word that is very important is "will". Will is the intention. It is the desire of the Wiccan. Almost everything in witchcraft has to do with making will come to reality. That means we cast most spells because we have desires that we need to come true. Fire is what sustains the desire. To work a spell, if you put in your heart and soul, if you're passionate about it, you're simply trying to tap into the amazing power of fire.

9. WATER

Water represents perseverance and quiet strength. It is the opposite of fire. While fire is violent and destructive, water is life-giving. Fire is flashy, but water is calm and reserved, flowing easily in its one direction. Water represents strength that is generated over time. It is a symbol of patience.

10. AIR

Air represents the spirit world. It stands for the unseen force that can be clearly felt. There are certain mysterious elements in the air that can awaken consciousness and place it in a divine place where wisdom is transmitted. Of all the elements, air is the only one that cannot be seen and yet we are very aware of its existence. This is because it can be clearly felt and is part of our existence. He explains that there are many things that are beyond the comprehension of human beings, but which actually play an important role in our lives. There are many symbols in the Wiccan world. So much that a book might not be able to cover all because of the minor diversities that Wiccans have in belief or manner of service. However, the ones listed above are the major ones that you are most likely going to come across within the first few minutes of your Wiccan experience. Only after you understand each symbol as well as the implications they hold can you apply them during spells or rituals. Whatever you want to do, it does not stop at understanding the symbols. Your will is key to your success as a Wiccan.

Also, you must know how to harness your Wiccan magic. Yeah, I just said "magic". Maybe you are not sure if there is a relationship between Wicca and Magic.

CHAPTER SUMMARY

Wicca centers around a lot of symbols, each of which is highly significant and necessary at one point or the other. You should learn what these symbols are as well as what roles they play in the Wiccan practices.

CHAPTER TWO.

AN OVERVIEW OF THE INSTRUMENTS USED IN WICCAN MAGIC

TAROTS, CRYSTALS, AND HERBS

You see, no matter how important everything else is to magical success, belief is the most crucial.

Dorothy Morrison

Becoming a Wiccan begins with a single decision but, more importantly, growing in it is quite a painstaking process. It is a journey that is not limited to a single phase of life, but transcends ages and lifetimes. It is a never-ending, yet fruitful journey. That you have stayed with me all through the discussions and revelations in this book so far subtly points to your readiness to make the best of your Wiccan journey. After all, what is the essence of a religion in which you cannot call the Spirit world to your service in order to lead a fulfilled life? Magick is one of the few ways by which you could make the best of your Wiccan journey. Thankfully, there are different versions of magic in Wicca for you to select from at each point in time in a bid to bring to reality your heart desires or effect the desired changes in your life. These include the popular candle magic, the ornamental crystal magic and the traditional herbal magic, each with its requirements, method of application, as well as instruments for manifestation.

To start with, tarot reading is not an exclusive preserve of Wicca. Individuals and other pagan and neopagan groups engage in tarot reading for their commercial purposes and for religious activities respectively. A few questions to be answered in order to grate your curiosity and usher you into tarot magic: What are tarot cards? What does tarot reading mean? How does tarot magic work in Wicca?

Tarot cards are simple cards that appear to the layman as mere game cards designed with funny images, but no, they definitely mean more than that! These are cards that were originally used as game tools but significantly became instruments of fortune-telling, divination, meditation, and for several other mystical purposes. Although the origin is difficult to trace, they are believed to have been founded in the Orient and brought to the West by the Romans. Again, this cannot be fully verified or accepted, as other sources claim that the cards are an intellectual property of Europe, although this seems unlikely to be the case. A collection of tarot cards is called a deck. Over the centuries, several decks have been developed with various names and purposes. Examples include the Robin Wood deck, the Rider-Waite Tarot, the Thoth deck, Deviant Moon Deck, English Magic Tarot, Chrysalis Deck, Golden Deck and, of course, the Witches Tarot and the Everyday Witch Tarot Deck, which are specifically designed for the Wiccan activities. Although these decks are slightly different in the image representation, they each consist of a total of 78 cards, the standard for every tarot deck, and the major and minor arcana. The major arcana are divided into four different suits of fourteen cards, which are called swords, coins, wands, and so on. The four suits are representative of the four classical elements — air, water, earth, and fire. The major arcana, also known as 'The Fool's Journey' comprises 22 named cards as follows: The Fool, The Magician, The High Priestess, The Emperor, The Priest, The Lovers, The Chariot, Justice, The Hermit, The Wheel of Fortune, Strength, The Hanged Man, Death, Temperance, The Devil, The Tower, The Star, The Moon, The Sun, The Day of Judgement and the World. Like every other card in the deck, each of these 22 cards has a meaning and significance in divination and fortune-telling.

Based on its spiritual significance, fortune tellers, among other groups of people, specialize in reading tarot cards, deciphering the significance they hold, and making meaning out of it to tell people what their future holds for them. This is an age-long practice that has continued to gain wide acceptance in diverse societies across the West, although it has been forbidden in some parts. For a Witch, however, tarot cards are much more significantly useful than just fortune-telling. Wiccans view tarot cards in an entirely different light and use them in peculiar ways, all revolving around magic. A sum total of these uses is known as the Tarot Magic. If you are a new Witch looking to understand the know-how of tarot magic, or you are already a practicing Witch hoping to develop your skills, this is the moment for you. In the next few paragraphs, I discuss the different ways of putting tarots to use in Wicca.

TO INTERPRET DREAMS

Dreams make up a part of the essential channels via which Wiccans reach out to the Spirit world, especially their deceased loved ones and their ancestors. Conversely, it is also the same channel by which those in the other realm reach across to the Witches on the physical realm. It is the belief that the veil which separates the physical world from the other world of the Spirits. As Wiccans perform rituals to the Spirits in request of one favor or another, dreams are one of the ways by which they obtain confirmation of their requests. This assures you that as a Witch, you are most likely to have dreams from time to time. While some dreams may be entirely positive, some could be otherwise. In the same vein, while some dreams are quite comprehensible, some are enigmatic and would require translation and explanations. This is the point where your tarot cards come in. Tarot Spread is a trusted method of seeking answers to puzzling dreams and is entirely easy to practice. All you need are Three Cards Spreads, and you should note your interpretation in a Book of Shadows. Despite its relative ease, however, using tarot for unveiling hidden meaning in dreams requires some practice you should get used to. This is because there is a thin line between consciousness and unconsciousness. More so, while you dream, you stand between two portals of existence. Most times, you realize that you forget a larger part of a dream just after waking. This could be overcome with conscious training of the mind and a couple of practical steps to document as best you can everything you remember from your dream, no matter how minute it may seem. Tarot images serve as stimuli to the symbols hidden in your subconscious mind. They help to create patterns through a mechanism that links what you see with what you can remember. To get the best out of tarot for dream interpretation, you should have a pen, a light and your book of shadows or other paper next to your bed so that it is easy for you to document everything you remember. As you do this continually, you would likely create a pattern from what you have written down. Describe all the details that you remember so you could match them perfectly when using the tarot cards for interpretation.

TO COMMUNICATE WITH THE SPIRIT WORLD

Reaching out to the supernatural world could be done in a number of ways, and using the tarot cards is just one other effective one. From time to time, we have the need to communicate our petitions to the Spirits or the souls of our ancestors. This process is called divination. Using your tarot deck is as productive as summoning the Spirits to the physical realm during rituals. The added advantage that comes with using cards is that you do not need to go through the rigors of invoking the Spirits using spells. With the help of tarot cards, you can communicate all that you need to. More so, using a tarot deck is much safer and less demanding than using an Ouija board, for example. All you need to do is get your deck fully set, clear it, enter into your sacred circle and mentally summon the Spirit or entity you wish to operate with. Go ahead and communicate with it as if it were physically present. As you ask questions or make petitions, do your reading simultaneously, and you will find the responses. At the end of the session, you would have received enough conviction on the outcome of your questions.

TO MANIFEST A DESIRE

Another important use to which you could choose to put your tarot magick is to bring fulfillment to your heart desires. This is one key aspect that Witches and non-Wiccans alike who have encountered and understood the use of the tarot magic benefit from it.

People continue to use tarot cards to add value and blessings of multiple forms to their lives, and you could enjoy the same benefits too. A tarot deck is a comprehensive unit that symbolizes virtually all that mankind can ever ask for. Simply pick any of the cards that match your desires. You could select a single card or select all the cards you want and make a spread with them. If you wish to make a spread, first pick a signifier card, that is, you. It is often recommended to pick 'The Magician', but again, remember that individuality comes first. You could pick any other one that appeals to you. After that, you then begin to select all the cards that symbolize your desires.

Whatever nature is, whether it is living or not, human or otherwise, or whether it is a situation or positive event that you wish to bring into reality, you will find a suitable card to represent it. After selecting all the cards that you want — and you're sure they represent just what you have in mind — you can make a spread of them and go ahead to charge the cards with Spirit. This can be done via means of chanting or prayers or any other suitable methods. Meditating on the cards for some time, with the conviction that they will yield the exact outcome that you want.

TO FOCUS DURING MEDITATION

Meditation is key to Wicca. It is a vital stage in the lifelong process of growing as a Witch. Meditation goes beyond physical rest of the body, but deepens the concentration of the mental faculties toward a particular direction, free from distractions. Tarot cards have been found to foster maximum focalization of the subconscious personality to enable you to reach onto higher planes of intuition, insight, and revelation. This is an endless journey into deeper meanings, because the more you dig in, the more of yourself you unleash. Again, meditation isn't a peculiar practice to Wicca. Members of other religions, such as monks, are also known for meditation. As a Witch, the tarot cards can help sharpen your meditation even more and make it super-productive. There are different methods of tarot meditation. You could spread the cards in front of you and select the one you need to actively connect with, or you let the tarot select for you by itself. Keep your eyes closed and your mind focused on the image of the particular card you are using to connect to the Spirit realm. Although meditation is a completely mental exercise, it begins with a physical step. I provide below a step-by-step guide to help you through tarot meditation.

SET THE PHYSICAL ENVIRONMENT

This should be the fundamental factor to put in place. Determine what setting you want to use for your meditation. It can be indoors or outdoors. Literally anywhere you can have absolute quiet. A place in nature such as a garden, beachside, mountain region, riverside, and other such areas are highly recommendable. After the location is sorted, select the time that aligns most with your meditation purpose, and keep away all distractions such as kids and gadgets, among others. You might want to play some soft meditation music in the background. You might want to burn some essential oils. Sit upright with your tarot deck placed right before you.

PICK A TAROT CARD

After settling yourself into a peaceful posture in a serene environment, it is necessary to pick a tarot card for meditation. This will be influenced by your purpose for meditation. If you are meditating simply to develop a better understanding of the tarot cards, you might want to select the card that appeals to you at that point in time or work by a preplanned order. But more importantly, if you are meditating for a particular purpose, it is advisable to pick a card that aligns with the said purpose. Again, you will always find one that matches your purpose.

SET YOUR GAZE ON YOUR TAROT CARD

At this point, you are gradually easing into a different state. Ensure that your mental focus is fully on the card you have placed before you. Think of nothing but the significance of the card and all of its representations. Think also of the purpose for which you chose the card and what impact that goal has on your life. From time to time, take slow deep breaths. Concentrate on the images in the card and begin to imagine them as items with life. Flow with the images in the card and allow them to resonate with you. After a while, you will find the objects in the image 'speaking' to you in special ways. This will create in your mind new meanings, insights and understanding. Upon attaining this peak, you are ready for awakening again. This is the stage at which you return from your journey into the supernatural realm. Meditation is not bound by a strict time rule. You can meditate for as long as the spirits urge you on.

TO WARD OFF NEGATIVITIES

Life is not always rosy, so you can expect to have negative feelings and ugly experiences from time to time. They may arise from an encounter with someone in a public place, or from an encounter with a surly boss or colleague at work, or from a quarrel with a family member, from bad dreams, and so on. However, just because you are aware of the inevitability of negativity does not imply that you should wish it away, but that you should prepare yourself to push it away as soon as it arrives. Whether it is negative feelings coming from your spirit or your mind, or even from external spirits, tarot magic is one of the reliable ways to keep them at bay.

Releasing a bad feeling takes almost the same process as meditation. The major difference lies in the cards that are selected. In this case, instead of choosing positive cards, you select negative cards that represent or at least relate to the feeling you want to get rid of. If you are not sure which cards to choose, you can let the tarot deck guide you.

Pentacles, for example, ward off financial problems and physical attacks, and Sword cards ward off criticism from others and judgment. Similarly, the suit of Cups protects you from negative emotional influences. After selecting your cards, place them face down, focus your gaze on it and begin your spells.

TO CAST SPELLS

Casting spells takes a central part of a Witch's life and activities. Spells are useful on various occasions and for diverse purposes. Common items used in spellwork are candles, herbs, and crystals, but what is unknown to most Wiccans is that the tarot deck in their custody can do the job of crystals, herbs, and candles in situations where they are absent. This is the explanation behind it: each of these three basic tools is an embodiment of spiritual images with the power to bring about the desired effect. The same can be said of tarot cards. Tarot cards are more like the low budget forms of these three major magick types. More so, all the 78 cards come with their respective representations, which could be about 156 if used in the reversed format. A single tarot card represents a goal, a simple spell or an intention that is as effective as the three main spell types.

In addition to serving as direct instruments for spells in exchange for the other methods which could be expensive to assemble and use, tarot cards could as well be used in addition to the other methods so as to determine the direction of the spell before its commencement and to confirm the success of the spell. This also applies to rituals. Tarot cards help to guide you through your ritual process. You simply need to do a card spread or ask direct yes or no questions.

The only major challenge you might be confronted with as a newbie in Wiccan tarot usage is knowing the system of the cards, what they represent as well as their significance. This is not difficult to understand. From constant use, you will grow into the workings of the card. Notwithstanding, I provide you with some basic general knowledge of some of the tarot cards and what they mean or symbolize

- **Cup Cards:** These relate to matters of love, affection, relationships, and family. Cards under this category are The Lovers card, which helps you decide which partner is better for you if you have two options; the Ace of Cups, which is used to mark a new beginning in a romantic affair, and the Queen of Cups, which signifies an erotic woman. Cup cards are also used to signify the Water element.

- **Sword Suit:** Cards in this suit include A Three of Swords, which symbolizes pain in a love triangle; The Knight of Swords, which unveils the truth always, and the Seven of Swords, which is used to represent a liar and deceiver. Sword cards are also used to signify the Air element.

- **Coin Cards:** These are generally cards used to symbolize one's economic welfare. The Eight of Coins stands for success in one's endeavors or promotion; the Ace of Coins represents financial prosperity or money magic, while the Page of Coins is used to bring an end to one's financial troubles. The Coin Cards are also used to signify the Earth element.

- **Wand Cards:** Cards in this category are the Three of Wands, which is used for representing long-sought success, and the Four of Wands, which signifies celebrations. Generally, this suit involves creativity. It also signifies the Fire element.

- **The Major Arcana:** This suit comprises cards that relate to the Spirit world. The Magician Card is used to master one's own spiritual affairs and destiny. The Death Card is used for spiritual rebirth; the Strength Card, as the name implies, is useful for spiritual fortitude. The Devil Card and Tower are somewhat negative in approach. They are used for laying curses. The Major Arcana symbolizes the Spirit element.

ANIMISM IN WICCA

I have left off this topic until this section to help you understand why tarot cards are so powerful and effective. The answer is simply animism!

Animism describes the belief that the supposedly inanimate items, places, animals, insects, human creations and the natural environment as a whole have a spirit and a soul. In simpler terms, animism holds that literally everything, whether living or not, is actually alive and possesses its own spirit. What started as a belief later grew into a religion on its own, which happens to be very similar but slightly different from spiritualism. Thereafter, it has come to be accepted by various neopagan religions but with diverse alterations.

What grew into animism definitely did not start as a religious concept, but as an anthropological idea, which was developed and popularized by Sir Edward Taylor in his 1871 book titled *Primitive Culture* in which he propounded that there is a pervading life force in natural things other than humans. However, it has been found that the idea was originally an idea of the primitive people who viewed themselves as contemporaries of the environment in which they live — the trees, plants, flowers, animals, rocks, rivers, and so on, hence they treated these natural creations with reverence. Today, animism has widened in scope and has assumed a supernatural dimension. Everything, man-made items such as desks, cars, chairs, and so on, natural things, animals and plants are now believed to have spiritual consciousness just like humans. Although some Wiccan covens have also adopted this belief, there are certain modifications. This is exemplified in the Wiccan respect for nature and the belief in the powers of tarot cards, for example.

Remember that our focus so far in this chapter is to establish the indispensability of tarots in Wiccan magic. Tarot magic is as important as candle magic, herbal magic, and crystal magic, and in fact, requires much less to undertake. While the major magick types necessarily involve a whole lot of magical tools to aid their efficiency and convey your desires to the Spirit world for fulfillment, all that you require to use the tarot magic is your tarot deck. What is even more vital about the tarot magick is that you can use it with the other magic types to guide you through the process, and provide answers to your questions when you are confused, as well as give confirmation to your practices. Furthermore, following the neo-pagan principle of animism, tarot cards not only symbolize spiritual bodies, but are themselves spiritual objects with souls of their own. This is a true statement, based on the fact that tarot cards have the ability to transform you from the physical to the spiritual realm during meditation and can give life to your heart's desires, among many other uses. Again, many types of tarot cards have been developed in the modern world, with a few differences from the original version of the deck. Notwithstanding, you should rely on your intuition when selecting one. It is highly recommendable that you opt for the Wiccan Tarot Deck as a Witch.

CHAPTER SUMMARY

Wicca relies heavily on the use of magical tools such as candles, crystals and tarot cards. Find all the know-how of the respective magical tools in this chapter.

CHAPTER THREE.

THE WICCAN SPELLS AND RITUALS

CONDUCTING YOUR PERSONAL WICCAN RITUAL

Through the Goddess, we can discover our strength, enlighten our minds, own our bodies, and celebrate our emotions.

Starhawk

One of the most endearing aspects of Wicca, which sells it out to non-Wiccans and specifically members of other religions, is the Wiccan ritual. Rituals are sacred occasions laden with both spiritual and ceremonial undertones. A ritual is one of the few occasions in Wicca when people gather for a collective goal.

These occasions include a betrothal (wedding), initiation, Sabbath, Esbat or a funeral, best considered as an end-of-life ceremony. In each of these occasions, the God and/or Goddess or both (depending on your Wiccan coven) play(s) a major role in the ritual process. This is because, like every other religion, the deities are at the center of every Wiccan ritual. It is important to state upfront that Wiccan rituals do not necessarily have to be public.

Whether public or private or exclusively personal, a ritual does not lose its spiritual significance. However, most covens choose to carry out their rituals in public view and may even invite non-Wiccans to participate for a couple of reasons. First off, this is in a bid to educate and enlighten the public on the practices of the group and also to address misconceptions trailing the religion. In addition, it is also a subtle way of making nonmembers who might be interested in joining the group learn about the activities by witnessing these rituals firsthand. Again, public rituals are not in any way compulsory. This means if you are not interested in public activities, you could choose to carry out these same rituals on your personal altar. It is my belief that a larger percentage of Wiccans find it more comfortable to carry out their rituals in private, so I provide in a latter part of this chapter the steps to guide you through conducting your personal Wiccan ritual successfully and without stress.

Rituals differ based on the occasion, purpose, covens, and nature, among many other factors. Some may be elaborate, especially the coven rituals practiced in public, while, on the other hand, some may be simple and quick, involving very few activities. While some public coven rituals involve specific steps known to their initiates, activities involved in personal rituals are often instinctive and unpredictable. More so, the content and activities in one ritual often differ from another and largely depend on the specific occasion at hand. Sabbats, for example, have a broader scope than Esbats and

Full Moon celebrations, as the former are occasions to recognize and honor the cooperative relationship between the Goddess and the God, as well as their impacts on the cycle of life, while the latter are intended exclusively to dignify the Goddess. As a matter of fact, it is almost impossible to find two Wiccan rituals that are exactly similar in all forms.

These differences, notwithstanding, there are a couple of steps and activities involved in a typical Wiccan ritual which must, as a matter of fundamental importance, be observed in every Wiccan ritual. In the next few paragraphs, I discuss these basic steps and activities, after which I walk you through the guides for conducting your personal ritual as a new Witch or initiate.

PURIFICATION

This is perhaps the first step after every tool and item needed for the ritual has been put in place. Purification involves cleansing the ritual participants of all negative energies that might hamper the success of the ritual. It also includes clearing off the adverse spirits in the atmosphere of the arena where the ritual is to be conducted. The items to be used for the ritual are not to be left out of purification. Purification could be done in quite a number of ways, but the simplest method is smudging, a process involving the burning of herbs such as lavender and rosemary, among others. The smoke emitted is believed to keep contrary spirits at par.

SETTING THE ALTAR

The altar may appear to be a mere physical setting, but it certainly has enough spiritual significance that you should keep this point in mind. It is important to prepare the altar whether it is a public or private ritual. For private rituals, it may be a little less demanding because you only have to do the main setup once and, thereafter, add the necessary tools for decoration, such as fall foliage depending on the ritual at hand. For public rituals, however, it is necessary to set up the ritual altar from time to time, also according to the demands of the ritual or the traditions of your Wiccan coven. Items for decorating the altar can range from fundamental symbols to tools such as crystals, wand, chalice, censer, and so on.

HOW TO SET YOUR PERSONAL WICCAN ALTAR

For the benefits of new Witches, I present to you a set of simple steps for setting your altar. Bear in mind that the steps provided here do not constitute a law of setting up your altar. They are the recommended basics, no doubt, but you could choose to remove one or two items from your own altar if you wish. After all, your altar should be representative of your personality, interests, goals and so on.

CHOOSE THE SURFACE OF YOUR ALTAR

The surface of your altar should be any raised platform on which you can place your tools and the likes. It is the seat of your Wiccan activities, spells and rituals. Recommendable options include a table, desk, stump, or any other platform with a similar surface. You should also cover the surface chosen with a tablemat or a cover cloth, if you wish.

DECIDE THE LOCATION OF YOUR ALTAR

For coven altars, this is not a difficult decision to make since it is always outdoors, but since yours is a personal altar, you have to decide if you want your altar outside in your compound or inside. It is advisable to set it in a secure corner indoor, but again, this is a decision you have to reach considering your apartment.

Once this has been done, you should also decide the orientation of your altar. In simple terms, do you want it positioned to the North, East, West or South? Aligning the altar towards the North is the most common practice among Wiccans.

DECORATE YOUR ALTAR WITH THE BASIC WICCAN TOOLS AND SYMBOLS

Once you have successfully positioned your altar, you should definitely decorate it. There are two kinds of items that should adorn your altar: basic traditional utensils and your personal decorative items. Traditional utensils are more or less unavoidable, but can be substituted with less expensive alternatives if you can't afford the actual items.

Below, I provide a list of these items and their respective worthy substitutes. The second group of items comprises items that make you feel at home. These can be jewelry, crafts, pictures, flowers, live plants, etc. Remember that the choice is yours. Below, you will find a list of the unavoidable items that must be on your altar, as well as items that you could use as substitutes in case you cannot find the actual items or they are over your budget.

TOOL	SUGGESTED REPLACEMENT
An image of the God or Goddess or both	A printed image if you can't afford a molded one.
The Pentacle	A paper or wood circle with the directions of the Pentacle drawn on it.
Chalice	Any cup at all will serve.
Cauldron	A heat-proof pot.
Athame	Knives
Wand	A stick
Censer	A pot, cup or bowlful of sand or salt.
Candles	Not quite expensive, but where none is available, the daylight will serve.
Broom	Always readily available
Incense	A basket of potpourri or a small dish of essential oils

To represent the elements of Air, Earth, and Fire, use a fan, a stone and a statue associated with fire respectively.

CASTING THE CIRCLE

This could be regarded as the final step before invocation. Why do you have to cast a circle around your altar as part of your ritual process? A sacred circle is essential to separate you both physically and spiritually from the mundane world. It serves more like a boundary that sets you apart and keeps distractions away. It also represents your transformation from the physical plane onto the supernatural. To cast your circle, you could use a long cord and mark with salt or stones or candles, as is available to you. Be sure to cast a pretty large circle to allow you sufficient room for movements around your altar.

INVOCATIONS

At this point, you are gradually entering the ritual process itself. What follows is to call the Quarters. This means to summon the Goddess and/or the God, depending on your personal belief or the goal of the ritual at that point in time. In addition to the deity or deities invoked, you will also invite each of the five elements — Earth, Air, Fire, Water and Akasha or Spirit. After successfully summoning these elements and the deities, and you can already feel their presence around, you can then go ahead to state your intentions. The intentions might be for ceremonial purposes, such as Sabbat or Esbat celebrations, or, on the other hand, to seek the help of the deities for one or two personal desires. Whatever the goal is, feel free to disclose it all at this point. In addition, spells come in handy at this point. After the ritual is completed, you necessarily have to thank the deities and the elements invited, with the strong conviction that your requests have been granted. In coven rituals, joy, dancing, clapping and singing are usually still dependent on the party in question, but in most personal rituals, this is usually not the case. However, one must close the circle and ground oneself, i.e. descend from the spiritual height that one has previously reached. There are different ways of grounding. Some people use crystals, while others prefer to do things that work with them, such as listening to music, singing or simply meditating. It is all a matter of personal choice.

On the overall, do bear in mind that rituals are diverse in forms, setups, and goals, so do not be amazed if you find a coven or another Witch conducting their rituals in ways that are slightly or completely different from the procedure provided here. The reason for the differences lies in the constantly changing nature of Wicca, a feature which owes to the fact that various versions of the 'religion' continue to sprout from time to time. As a result of this, several covens and Wiccan groups have developed their respective modus operandi. Above all, remember that there is no specific binding guidebook to the Wiccan practices as a whole. This means you should do what works for you. Allow your spirit to flow with your ritual and every step involved. This way, you can rest assured that you will get the desired outcome.

On a final note, as a new Wiccan, you are most likely going to encounter difficulties, seeming failures, fears and doubts about yourself as you begin your rituals and other Wiccan practices. This is only natural and expected. Donald Michael Kraig has this to say, *No one can give you magickal powers. You have to earn them. There is only one way to do this. Practice, practice, practice!*

CHAPTER SUMMARY

What is Wicca without the spells and rituals? This chapter dwells on the steps involved in carrying out Wiccan rituals and also teaches you the tools required to carry out your personal ritual in your closet.

CHAPTER FOUR.

SELECTING CRYSTALS FOR WICCAN MAGICK

Magic is the science and art of bringing about change according to the will.

Aleister Crowley

Starting off a magical activity could seem magical to you as a Wiccan newbie, and that's perfectly understandable. Magic requires a carefully detailed process that may comprise diverse tools, including spells, tarots, wands, stones, herbs, and even candles. This explains that there are different types of magic, but the most commonly recognized ones in Wicca are candle magick, herbal magic, and the beautiful crystal magic. In this chapter, I discuss with you the nature and potency of crystal magic, the magical properties of crystals as well as how to apply them in Wicca, but even before I delve into these details, it is necessary for you to understand what these crystals or precious stones are outside magic, as well as how they are formed. You would have to relax your mental cells at this point because the world of crystals is both interesting and demanding. Some of the information I will give you in this chapter may be too much for you as a new or potential sorcerer, especially if you are completely new to the world of stones or have only been fascinated by them from afar but without any level of knowledge. Whichever category you fall into, this chapter will address your knowledge gap and equip you well enough to become an expert in crystal magic.

WHAT ARE CRYSTALS?

Crystals are solid materials made from millions of atoms and organic, and sometimes inorganic, minerals that are arranged in dimensions. Organic crystals are naturally formed in the death crust and may take several years to fully solidify. A typical example of organic crystals is the clear Quartz. On the other hand, most crystals are rather artificial, that is, formed through a variety of crystallization processes.

Crystals come in diverse shapes and colors, and this owes to the different molecules involved in the formation process, as well as the natural or chemical actions that occurred during the process. While some have flat surfaces and pointed edges, some are rough, rocky and round.

Typically, the structure of a crystal itself is determined by the spatial arrangement of the unit cells, each of which contains atoms in various numbers arranged in a particular order. It is these unit cells that are further arranged in a three-dimensional form to result in what we know as crystals. Ordinarily, crystals are charged with electrical, mechanical, vibrational and optical properties, which make them useful for various purposes such as channels of electrical power and for mechanical use as in wristwatches. It is these natural energies that

Wiccans and other practitioners tap into for spiritual goals such as healing, protection, good luck, and other magical ends. As a matter of fact, there are certain special practitioners other than Witches who capitalize on the vibrational powers of crystals for therapeutic purposes.

This is summarized as crystallotherapy. Such acts of healing are made possible as the stones interact with and awaken the natural energies within a person. It will interest you to learn that this crystal healing has been in practice for a long, and you can already guess why it still is. It is effective!

Of course, if it wasn't, Wiccans would have no business using crystals for whatever reasons. An interesting spiritual dimension to stones is that they are also connected to each of the five elements, which work together to charge them (the crystals) with life and energy. Hence, Witches believe that whether natural or artificially made, crystals are alive, and this is not without basis.

Have you ever tried holding a crystal in your palm for a few moments? It wouldn't be long before you begin to sense the vibrational charge. In addition to the vibrations, the many beautiful colors of crystals are quite appealing to the eyes and may be used for decorative purposes as jewelry, at homes and on Wiccan altars, but it definitely goes beyond mere decoration!

The crystal colors have a spiritual significance, which Wiccans deploy for rituals, healing, protection, good luck, meditation, and so on.

USES OF CRYSTALS IN WICCA

Having already established that crystals are predominantly used outside Wicca in various ways that may be therapeutic or even economic in orientation, it is high time we domesticated crystals to Wicca. It is no doubt that Witches explore the natural powers of crystals for spiritual purposes, the question is, how exactly do they do this? I dwell on this very briefly.

TO FOCUS ENERGIES

The most foundational use of crystals in Wicca is to focus the supernatural energies during rituals especially. Bear in mind that crystals are symbolic of the five elements of the universe. Using the crystals summons these elements to your activity for a start. In addition, they seem to draw the presence of the spiritual deities to your altar. Some persons prefer to place crystals such as Clear Quartz and Amethyst. They also help you to focus your inner energies on the ritual process.

FOR CHAKRA WORK

For Witches who believe in chakra healing, the crystals come in handy a lot. Chakras are believed to be the energy channels in the subtle body of every individual. These seven energy channels could get blocked or imbalanced due to several natural and spiritual reasons. When such happens, crystals, being packed with energies themselves, could be used to open up the blocked chakras or align them as the case may be. Red Jasper, for example, could be used to heal the Mulhadara chakra; Tiger's Eye for the Sacral chakra; Citrine for the Manipura chakra; Malachite for the Anhata Chakra; Azurite for the Vishudda chakra; Blue tourmaline for the Ajna chakra, and Calcite for the Sahasrara chakra. Note that there are lots of other stones for healing each of the seven chakras. The ones provided here are simply some out of many. If you are interested in chakras, you might want to read up on them

USED IN SPELLS

Specific stones are very useful for conjurations and spells in Wicca. Rose Quartz, for example, is very essential for spells related to love, happiness, and forgiveness. In addition, selenite has the power to connect you to the spirit world during spellcasting and to recharge you for full connection to the supernatural.

FOR MEDITATION AND FOCUS

Meditation requires full focus, a state which might be humanly impossible to achieve even after you have sorted out the physical environment and you are in a comfy arena. It might still be difficult to focus because of the mental images of past experiences and negative encounters that might begin to pop up on your mind. Sometimes, more so, the inability to focus during meditation is a consequence of negative spirits around. Having crystals around will solve the problem for you. Merely holding a crystal-like turquoise helps you relax and brings you the inner peace you need to focus on your meditation.

FOR SPECIFIC MAGICAL PURPOSES

Crystals are quite excellent items for decoration, but for a Witch, they certainly mean much more than that. The beautiful stones have great magical value as they are useful for various purposes in magic depending on their inherent proprieties such as energy, shape, and color. Such functions include honoring deities, casting spells, meditation, protection, healing, good luck, success in one's business, financial breakthrough, love and attraction, making wealth rituals, and so many others. The list is almost endless. In a latter part of this chapter, I provide in detail some of the magical functions of a handful of stones used in Wicca.

TO CONDUCT DIVINATIONS

Divination is pivotal to the success of many Wiccan activities, rituals especially. It is one of the ways of consulting and communing with the deities to foresee the events to happen and to understand the state of things revolving around a Witch at the moment. Divination is one of the strengths of a Wiccan because it gives an assurance that you are still on the right path and in a favorable relationship with your deities. What is sweeter than hearing from your personal gods and seeing signs from them?

TO MARK THE SACRED CIRCLE

Another similarly important way crystals are used in Wicca is to draw the Sacred circle. The sacred circle is the section drawn around the Wiccan altar to keep the witch separate from the mundane world and, spiritually, to transform the witch from the physical realm to the supernatural, where most Wiccan operations are performed. The circle also serves to keep the altar from unwanted spirits and to keep the Witch focused during meditation.

TO DECORATE MAGICAL TOOLS

This is perhaps one of the least known uses of crystals. It is already established that crystals have inherent magical abilities. In some traditions, Witches tap into these powers to strengthen their magical tools for magic and rituals. For example, some stones are seemingly used to decorate tools like the wand and the pentacle, but in essence, it goes beyond decoration. The stones attached to such items help to strengthen and reaffirm their significance in the magic world. In other words, stones aid the functionality of these tools.

WORN AS MAGICAL JEWELRY OR CHARMS

This is perhaps the least demanding and most unsuspecting way to use your crystals. Drawing on the appealing outlook of crystals, you could make them into jewelry in the form of simple necklaces, wristlets, earrings, waist beads, and so on. The public thinks they are mere fanciful items, but they definitely do more than that! The wonderful thing about this method is that you can wear them anywhere, almost 24 hours of the day! Now that you know some of the general uses of crystals, what's next? It is high time you picked your own crystals at will. Let's walk you through a list of the most commonly used crystals and their functions and how to use them.

CLEAR QUARTZ

Clear Quartz is basically one of the most common stones out there. It has been in use for a long, dating back to the ancient Greek who named it *krystallos* meaning ice because they thought it was ice stones from the gods. It is purely organic, very much available in the Earth's crust and can be found in almost every part of the world.

An interesting thing about clear quartz is that, in addition to its availability, it is useful for multiple purposes both within and outside Wicca. In fact, it has been considered a universal stone because it is useful where there are no other stones. It is especially useful for protection, clarity and healing spells.

SELENITE

Selenite is a transparent and colorless crystalline material and a variety of gypsum. This is why it is also known as gypsum flower or satin spar. Although selenite is basically colorless, some varieties come in colors of orange, grey, green or brown but are all definitely transparent.It can be used for healing blocked energy channels, clarity of mind during meditation and spells, for increasing awareness of oneself, to gain access to the spirit guides, to aid assessment, judgment, and insight and to clear the confusion. Some Witches have reported that selenite is also useful for creating and understanding dreams.

AMETHYST

Amethyst is a necessary crystal for scrying into the future because it helps to clear one's psyche, sharpen the intuition and enhance one's ability to focus. It can as well be used as a natural tranquilizer because it relieves pain, stress, irritability, anger, hatred, and anxiety. It also helps to reduce addictions, check dangerous and detrimental behaviors, as well as eliminate the effects of alcohol. More so, it is a stone known to alleviate sicknesses, especially mental ailments. During rituals and festivals, Wiccans use it to clear the arena because it also possesses strong cleansing powers. In addition, it activates your spiritual consciousness, opens up your psychic abilities for deeper meanings.

HEMATITE

Hematite is a product of iron oxide mineral, which can be predominantly found in rocky areas. It comes mainly in dark colors, which include black, brown, reddish-brown, silver-gray or stark red. It is especially useful for grounding after meditations or rituals. This is because it helps to strengthen the connection with the Earth element and provides safety, security, and endurance. Hematite is also useful for concentration, as it further enhances your mental performance and makes you stay focused. For some people, hematite is a tool for good luck, especially in legal cases. It also has effects on the physical body, as it helps balance the nervous system, and on mental health, as it increases self-esteem.

GREEN JADE

There are several types of jade, but the green jade stands out among all for its amazing ability to heal emotional imbalance. It is considered a dream stone because it grants access to the spirit world and gives insight into rituals.

Jade bestows long life on its possessor and aids early recovery from infirmities. It is a stone of friendship and good luck. It promotes love and both interpersonal and intrapersonal understanding. It gives wisdom and clarity, improves your emotional state, and strengthens the power of love. It also dispels negative energy.

AGATE

Agate is one of the most essential stones in crystal magic. Especially useful for casting spells, it helps to restore all lost energy and could also be useful for therapeutic purposes. It provides a relaxing experience, sporadically increases creativity and intellectual abilities, hence it is used for children and teenagers, who are still in their developmental stage. It is connected to the earth element, and as a result, makes you feel safe and grounded. This explains why it is used in spells meant for protection too.

ROSE QUARTZ

Rose quartz is a variety of quartz that gets its name from the rosy pink hue of the stone. This color is a result of the presence of some atoms of titanium in the crystal. Sometimes, the color could change to rose-red, rose-pink or a faint purple. It is the crystal of love, a belief that is not far from the fact that it is often shaped in the form of the heart. If you are interested in finding love from others or self-love, you should consider the rose quartz. It is also known to resolve inner troubles, feelings of anxiety, tension, and heartbreak and bring peace instead. More so, rose quartz wards off negativity, hatred and makes you embrace trust and acceptance, both of yourself and others.

CITRINE

Here is one stone everyone who believes in the power of crystals should have. It helps in many great ways. If you have problems with expressing yourself convincingly or you suffer an inferiority complex or lack of confidence, you should consider keeping this stone within reach. It provides you with the needed confidence to communicate effectively with others in the family, at social circles and at work. It also clears off negative energy and keeps your day bright and positive all along.

CARNELIAN

Carnelian is an orange stone believed to turn ideas into reality. It comes in handy a lot for Witches because of its transformative powers. It gives light, warmth, and comfort. Some persons also wear it for motivation and courage and for success in their business endeavors because it drives goals into reality. You can make it into a necklace or wrist chain and wear it about always.

SODALITE

Sodalite is a crystal blend of different blue hues and white. Witches and non-Wiccans alike wear it to promote intelligence, communication, cooperation, knowledge, rationality, and learning. It is great to wear while working in a group or in situations where you would need to communicate your ideas as well as understand other peoples' points of view. Sodalite is the stone of wisdom, learning, and study. More so, it is associated with logic and intellect and promotes control over one's own mind. Sodalite clears mental noise so inner calm can blossom and clears the way for your self-awareness and self-improvement.

It would turn out an endless and needless exercise to attempt to list out all the possible crystals that you might come across in your Wiccan journey and experience. More so, you would not need all of them at a time, so memorizing the uses and properties of each stone won't do you much good. The most important point to note at this stage is that crystal magic is quite effective and harmless to use. At least, no stone threatens as much as some herbs. From time to time, you would have the need to use one stone or the other. Be sure to make a comprehensive check on the particular stone you are about to use in order not to misapply them. To wrap up this chapter, I provide a few tips on the use of crystals in Wicca.

CLEANSE YOUR CRYSTALS

Remember that crystals operate basically on vibrational energies. As effective as this is, it has its own downside — accumulating negative energies when not in use. These adverse energies could hinder your stones from functioning as intended or work completely against you. It, therefore, becomes a necessity to always cleanse your stones before you use them. How do you clean? Leave them outside in the sun, or more effectively, smudge them!

WEAR CRYSTALS EVERY DAY

This is not something demanding. For crystals like Jade, Clear Quartz, Citrine and others that influence your daily life and activities, carrying them around is the best way for them to be effective. You can leave them in your bags, purses or anything else with you. You can also wear them as necklaces or bracelets. That's like wearing a beautiful piece of jewelry. Simple but effective!

USE CRYSTALS WITH OTHER MAGIC METHODS

Yes, it can be done. Combining two or more methods of magic, especially on serious Wiccan occasions, is much more effective than using just one. To do this, all you need to do is to align your stones with the other method, be it a candle or herbs. Remember that each of the elements of the respective methods has its own uses. Don't mix herbs with candles of different purposes, and never use the wrong stone with the wrong herb.

Thousands or Wiccans and millions or non-Wiccans are benefiting from crystal magick all over the world. Use the stones for your own good too, bless them!

CHAPTER SUMMARY

It's time to get detailed! You learned briefly the different types of magic that obtain in Wicca. Crystal magic is one of the most common. Learn how to use crystals for the realization of your wishes here.

CHAPTER FIVE.

WHEEL OF THE YEAR: THE WICCAN FESTIVALS AND CELEBRATIONS

Wicca all year long. A brief introduction to the Wicca Wiccan practices, beliefs as well as the Wiccan festivities and sabbats is a good place to start.

Wicca is commonly described as a non-organized religion since it has no designated place of worship, no central holy text and there are no standard ritual proceedings to observe. All of these details are better decided by individual traditions, covens and solitary practitioners. Despite this flexible nature of the Wicca religion, one very important element of the Wicca religion that serves as a structural center for the religion is the *Wheel of the year*.

There are thousands of different Wiccan groups in the world and while there is no one governing body over Wicca, there are a few ideas and practices common to almost all modern Wicca groups. It is important to note that not all pagans are Wiccans and not all pagan traditions have the same principles as the beliefs of contemporary Wicca.

THE PAGAN WHEEL OF THE YEAR

The wheel of the year represents the eight pagan holidays or Wiccan sabbats. These sabbats are celebrated as holidays to honor and celebrate the seasons and cycles of life for pagans and Wiccans. Even those who are not of these spiritual beliefs recognize these holidays in various ways, as Wicca is, in fact, considered an earth-based religion. Pagan cosmology is cyclical as are the other Eastern religions - all things are in a perpetual cycle of birth, death and rebirth. Paganism relates this cycle to the annual progression of the seasons, as well as the waxing and waning of the sun. Pagan festivals align with days marking key points in the annual cycle, especially the beginning and climax of the four seasons.

These holidays represent the start of each season and mid-way points between them and are evenly split throughout the year. They are called pagan holidays as they have their roots in the pagan religions of the Celtic and Germanic pagans, and as such Wiccans observe these holidays as Sabbats. Although the word Sabbath is more associated with Judaism and Hebrew, in the Wiccan religion it is called Sabbat, which refers to a gathering or meeting of people to practice rituals and rites. Pagan holidays and Sabbaths are used interchangeably, as they represent the same days on which their festivals and ritual celebrations take place. There are eight holidays celebrated throughout the pagan traditions. Each holiday is celebrated with a community festival and season-appropriate rituals. These festivals are depicted visually via the wheel of the year symbol. This wheel is a modern innovation shaped like an eight-armed sun cross. Most people often wonder where the wheel starts due to the fact that its shape is circular and round objects usually don't have an end or a beginning. Some people believe that the new cycle begins on Samhain since it is the witches' New Year, while some others believe that it falls on or after Yule since it corresponds with modern calendars. Each segment of the wheel represents six or seven weeks. Four points are based on the solar calendar: the winter and summer solstice as well as the spring and autumn equinox, while the other four points are based on Celtic festivals and are often referred to by their Celtic names: Imbolc, Beltane, Lughnasadh, and Samhain. The eight holidays go by different names depending on your location and tradition. The wheel of the year holidays originates mostly from both Celtic and Germanic pagan rituals. Some of these holidays were celebrated by the Celtic pagans, while the others were celebrated by Germanic pagans. Some people believe that the eight holidays were melded together to become what is now known as the wheel of the year. The pagan holidays were not only split between The Celts and the Germans but also according to greater and lesser sabbats. The lesser sabbats fall between solstices and equinoxes and were deeply rooted in the Germanic pagan religious celebrations. They are:

- Yule

- Ostara

- Litha

- Mabon

The greater sabbats fall in between the cross-quarter days and were deeply rooted in the Celtic pagan traditions. They are:

- Imbolc

- Beltane

- Lughnasadh

- Samhain

Here are the holidays:

WINTER SOLSTICE (YULE)

The winter solstice is usually 12 o'clock on the pagan wheel of the year. The Norsemen of northern Europe saw the sun as the wheel changed the seasons. The word "Yule" is believed to have originated from "houl" which was used to refer to the wheel of the year. The Norsemen celebrated this holiday like all others with bonfires, storytelling, and feasting. The Romans, however, considered it the high point of their week-long Saturnalia festivities, during which they decorated their homes with greenery, lit candles and exchanged gifts.

Celtic druids burned Yule logs during this time to banish darkness and any evil spirits that might accompany it.It is usually celebrated during the winter when our days become shorter. It is a time in which preparations were made for the coming cold months and to remember the life-giving source of the sun as well as the warmth the sun provides. Trees are usually decorated with ornaments and foods that thrive in the cold months as a symbol of continual growth and life through the cold nights. Even some Christmas traditions come from Yule celebrations, including the use of mistletoes and the use of Yule logs to banish evil spirits and bring good luck. The Yule is one of the oldest winter traditions in the world and is usually held on the shortest day of the year. The day marked the death and rebirth of the sun, and it was celebrated more domestically than the summer solstice. It is usually celebrated from December 20 -23.

IMBOLC

The Imbolc is usually at 2 o'clock on the pagan wheel of the year. It is also called Disablot, Brigid's Day or Candlemas. Imbolc usually comes at the first sign of spring, a period where food supply from the previous harvest is running low. The word Imbolc literally translates to "in the belly" in Gaelic. It is usually called Imbolc because it is the period when the sheep first began to give milk again, signifying that they're pregnant. This holiday is of great importance and significance for a successful new farming season, as well as ensuring the earth provides enough food supply to last them till the next harvest. It is a joyous occasion that symbolizes the promise of the return of spring and is halfway between the winter solstice and spring equinox. It is time in which crops and animals are blessed to ensure an abundant year of good health and that new life would spring forth soon.

The Imbolc celebrations were centered on the lightening of fires like most of the other Celtic festivals. Fire was believed to be more important on this holiday than on others, as it also celebrated the holy day of Brigid, also known as Bride, Brigit or Brid, the goddess of fire, healing and fertility. Maidens and the pagan goddess Brigid are honored on this particular holiday, as they are symbols of fertility. After the conversion to Christianity in Ireland, the goddess Brigid became Saint Brigid and missionaries began to incorporate traditional pagan customs into Christianity in Ireland. The lighting of the fires was to celebrate the increased power of the sun in the coming months. It is usually celebrated on the 2nd of February.

VERNAL EQUINOX (OSTARA)

Ostara is usually at 3 o'clock on the pagan festival wheel. It celebrates the renewal of life on earth with the coming of spring. It is usually considered a time for rejuvenation and child-like wonder at the glories of the earth. It is sometimes coincidentally celebrated with festivals fro Aphrodite, Hathor, Ostara, and Easter. The days are becoming longer and warmer, and fertility is abounding. Fertility is represented with Eggs and hares – the origins of Easter traditions come from this holiday. It is usually celebrated from the 19th of March to 22 in the present day.

BELTANE

It is usually 4 o'clock on the pagan festival wheel. It also has many, including May Eve, Roodmas, Shenn do Boaldyn or Celtic May Day. The word "Beltane" means "Fires of Bel" in the language of the Celts and refers to the ancient Celtic deity of the same name. The spring fire festival celebrates the coming of the summer as well as the fertility of plants and animals of the coming year. It is an exciting time for celebration because spring is now full of bloom and much longer and warmer days are coming. The fire also plays a major role in Beltane than in any other pagan holiday, as it is their belief that fire cleanses and revitalizes. It is usually celebrated on the 1st of May in the present-day calendar. It is considered a time to give gratitude and thanks to the fertility of spring. Festivities usually start on the eve of the 1st of May with big beautiful bonfires lit to represent life and end on the 1st of

May with people wearing flower crowns and dancing the maypole. Cows are paraded between two bonfires to ensure strength and fertility for the herd and for this reason; some people also jump over a flame to increase fertility, which could either be physical, mental or creative in this case. Most of the Beltane rituals revolve around the needs of farming communities looking forward to a fruitful year ahead. As far as fertility goes, it is also a time where many marriages are arranged. Beltane was a time for celebrating and nurturing the harvest.

SUMMER SOLSTICE

The summer solstice is usually 6 o'clock on the pagan wheel and is known by many names, including Midsummer's Eve, Gathering Day, Litha, Alban Heffyn and Feill-Sheathai. As the Winter solstice, the summer solstice is about celebrating the power of the sun – the only difference is that during the winter solstice, the pagans miss the sun and are wishing it would come back, but during the summer solstice, they're honoring the sun while it is at the peak of its glory. Bonfires and feasting were the most common ways of celebrating this holiday, and this festival was much more public than the winter solstice. On this day also, the Chinese celebrate Li, the goddess of light, while the Christians celebrate St. John the Baptist. It is usually celebrated from the 19th of June to 23. Traditional methods of celebration include bonfires and torchlight processions, rituals to encourage the sun whose power will wane throughout the remainder of the season, which is why pagans refer to Litha as Midsummer.

LUGHNASADH

This festival is usually 7 o'clock on the pagan festival wheel and is also sometimes referred to as Lammas and Frey Feast. This festival is the midway point between summer and autumn and also traditionally marks the first day of harvest and commemorates the death of Lugh, the Celtic god of light, the son of the sun. Lugh is believed to be the medium through which the power of the sun can enter the grain and open it. In the mythological tale of the Wheel of the year, the god of the sun known as the sun god transfers his power into the grain and is sacrificed when the grain is harvested and so they have a dying, self-sacrificing and resurrecting god of harvest who dies so his people may live and not die of starvation. It is usually celebrated on the 1st of August. According to legend, Lugh's mother Tailtiu cleared the lands of Ireland to prepare for the planting of crops.

AUTUMNAL EQUINOX

Also referred to as Mabon and Harvest Tide, this festival is marked by 9 o'clock on the wheel of the year. This festival is considered a time for reflection of the past summer and preparation for the coming winter. It is a time when the waning power of the sun becomes very obvious. However, it is necessary to give thanks for the food obtained during the harvest, otherwise there will be no abundance of food in the next harvest. It is celebrated from September 21 to 24.

SAMHAIN

This festival is fondly addressed by many names, including Winter Nights, Halloween, Hallows, Hallow tide, Shadow Fest, Allan tide, Third Harvest, Harvest Home, Geimredh, Day of the Dead, Spirit Night, Candle Night, November Eve, Nut crack Night, Ancestor Night and apple fest. It is usually marked by 10 o'clock on the pagan wheel. This festival is done to celebrate the end of the harvest as well as the end of the summer and the beginning of the winter. It is also a festival for the dead and is marked by being a time when the veil separating the mortal and spirit worlds is at its thinnest allowing the souls of the dead, witches and creatures of all kinds to mingle with the living. The mingling of the dead with the living is not considered a mournful moment, but a time when departed loved ones are invited to join in the end of harvest celebrations and charged with the responsibility of watching over the new members of the community.

Jack o' lanterns are lit to light the way for the dead souls. It is time when one asks for guidance, help, clearing of negativity as well as preparing for the start of a new year in a positive light. Some worshipers even believe that this time is a period for magic. The Druids, in particular, believed that they could see into the future on this day as a result of the thinness of the veil that separates the world of the living from the dead. It is usually celebrated from the 31st of October to the 1st of November. These are just brief explanations of these amazing pagan holidays. They are rich in wonderful traditions, foods, crafts, and gatherings of their own. As you can see, there is a clear distinction between two sets of four festivals that have been blended together to give us the eight we have today. The seasons and the astronomical position of the sun during the solstices and equinoxes occur all over the world, so there are several similar celebrations of this type all over the world. These festivals or feasts are not entirely just pagan festivals or Wiccan sabbats nor are they celebrated only by pagans or Wiccans. Many ancient cultures and civilizations would have celebrated and honored these festivals in one way or another, as they are natural events.Every season has expectations or intentions that resonate with that particular time of the year. Winter is a time for reflection over the past and to learn from them as well as contemplate the future. Spring is a time to set new goals in motion as well as new ideas and intentions into our lives. Summer is a time to reflect on expectations and to free ourselves from things that will not bring us a good harvest. Autumn is a period of harvest and a time where we are able to see the fruit of our labors.

CHAPTER SUMMARY

Like every other religion, Wicca has moments of festivals and celebrations which, together, are called the Pagan Wheel of the Year. This chapter chronicles these annual and monthly celebrations and their significance for you as a Witch.

CONCLUSION

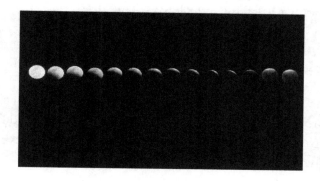

I hope this book has been of great benefit to you, and you have been able to learn a lot about Wicca, the mission was to guide you and nurture you with basic knowledge so you can start in this wonderful world. As a conclusion I would like to give you some basic principles that are clear in your mind.

BASIC PRINCIPLES OF THE WICCA RELIGION

Part of the beliefs of the Wiccan religion revolve around the following principles:

1. Nature is the object of worship. For Wiccans, nature is an object of worship, unlike monotheistic religions that worship the creator entity. As all elements of reality are considered divine, they do not conceive a separation between the divine and nature. Even in Wicca, it is presumed that each person harbors the divinity within him or herself.

2. They believe in the Threefold Law. Wiccans believe that everything that is done comes back to the person in triplicate. Therefore, they do not use their magical rituals to do harm. The principle is summarized as: everything that does not harm the other is lawful and allowed. Therefore,

3. Truth and morality are relative concepts. This also implies that the contribution of each participant must be valued.

4. They believe in magic, which they call "magick". They introduce the letter "K" at the end of the word to differentiate it from illusionism. Wiccans believe they can intervene in the natural order through rituals and esoteric practices.

5. They recognize the equity between women and men. In this sense, they believe in duality and balance.

6. They do not recognize organizational hierarchies. For this reason, the Wicca ritual is celebrated in a circle.

7. The main celebration is known by the name of coven, sabbat or coven, generic names that designate the meeting of witches.

WICCA
FOR BEGINNERS

The Ultimate Guide To Wiccan Beliefs And History, Magic, Witchcraft, Candles, Crystals, Runes, Herbs And Magic Rituals

Antony Vithale

INTRODUCTION

Wicca has remained to date a subject of mystery to many due, in part, to its sensitive and somewhat occultic nature and practices. As a result, the subject has sparked lots of interest across time and space among scholars, curious individuals and, yes, persons who are interested in the Wiccan practice of magic and spells.

It seems that the questions bordering Wicca are endless, and this is a reflection of the magnitude of interest it has garnered over time. With this book in your hand, you are most definitely interested in Wicca too. It doesn't matter if your interest is based on a desire to practice witchcraft or exercise your magical powers, or in an attempt to understand a Wiccan family member or friend, or if you are already in

144

the practice and wish to broaden your understanding of the practice. Whatever your purpose might be, this book aims to answer all your questions, resolve all misconceptions, clarify your doubts, gratify your curiosity and ultimately increase your knowledge of the subject matter. As Wicca is simple to understand but complex in its own way, this book has been delimited into parts and chapters for easy navigation.

However, before we delve into a detailed exploration of the subject matter, I intend to 'whet your appetite' in this introductory section by providing brief and random answers and explanations to some of the questions posed above. If I may start with the last question — is Wicca the same as paganism? —, the simplest way to put it is that all Wiccans are pagans, but not all pagans are Wiccans. This definitely leads us to the added question, what is paganism? For now, we may take paganism as any form of religion that believes in more than one god and often involves rituals. I must mention here, however, that most neopagan religions are now monotheist. Based on this, we can establish that while Wicca may be described as a pagan religion (if at all it is a religion per se), it does not exactly mean that it is the only pagan religion in existence. It is common for Wicca to come to mind when a mention of paganism is made, but this does not imply that all pagans are Wiccans. As a matter of fact, there are many other pagan religions, some of which are Kemetic, Norse Heathens and Classical Reconstructionists.

That settled, we can move on to another equally vital question, do all Wiccans practice witchcraft? A quick analogy here: do all doctors treat the teeth? Do all teachers teach Creative Arts? Do all transport workers drive long buses? Obviously, the answer to each of these illustrative questions is in the negative. If I should ask you why the answer is no, you might be forced to say, out of irritation, *Come on! Because they chose not to!* Yet, it goes without mention that not being a dentist doesn't make a doctor any less of a professional doctor, and not driving a long bus doesn't make anyone less of a transport worker, and at the same time, not teaching Creative Arts does not make one any less of a professional teacher. Based on this, we can, therefore, establish that practicing witchcraft does not make a Wiccan! It is only one of the added perks of being a Wiccan. This implies that not all Wiccans exercise witchcraft powers. I must admit that, from popular opinion, witchcraft is almost always interchanged for Wicca, but this is a rather misplaced position. A Wiccan can choose not to practice witchcraft. As a matter of fact, practicing witchcraft is just one out of the many sides to being a Wiccan, even though most Wiccans practice witchcraft in one form or the other. Notwithstanding, this does not imply that all those who practice witchcraft are Wiccans. Far from it! At this point, it is necessary, for the purpose of clarification, to shed some light on witchcraft as a practice.

In its broadest sense, witchcraft refers to all supernatural practices, including spellcasting, spirit communication, trance journeying, divination, and interaction with unseen forces, among several others, often with the purpose of causing effects on the physical world. Admittedly, the effect caused by witchcraft powers may not always be good or positive, and this is where 'black magick' and 'white magick' come in. So, while it is undeniable that witchcraft is a core aspect of Wicca, we must be generous enough to understand that they are two different things entirely. You could possibly be a Wiccan without being a witch, and on the other hand, you could be a witch without necessarily being a Wiccan. What is more? Wicca emphasizes more important practices such as devotion, connection with Nature, one's forbear and the Gods over practicing witchcraft. Another similarly important clarification that ought to be done at this point is that most Wiccans, both male and female, call themselves Witches (note the uppercase W) as a title for practicing Wicca, not witchcraft. The reason behind this is not far-fetched. The words 'Wicca' and 'Witch' originate from the same Anglo-Saxon word, which means *the wise one*. This largely accounts for the misconception that being a Wiccan automatically means being a witch. I shed more light on this in a later part of this book.

So far, I seem to have left off the most basic of all questions revolving around Wicca, which is, what exactly is Wicca? A cautious reader will have noticed that, so far, I have made no attempt to discuss the nature of Wicca as a subject. This is intentional! If you have made it this far, it is an indication that your curiosity hasn't been sated yet, and that is expectedly so. Enough of the tips. Let's delve into the real deal! In the next section of this book, I provide an in-depth exploration of the meaning, nature, and evolution of Wicca. You had better brace up, for the ride into an exploration of Wicca is about to get pretty interesting!

CHAPTER ONE.

THE TRUTHS ABOUT WICCA

WHAT IS WICCA?

It may be difficult to peg the concept of Wicca to one single definition, especially due to the fact that it is viewed differently by different persons from divergent perspectives. For example, a non-Wiccan scholar may consider it a set of pagan practices, while a non-Wiccan layperson may consider it the practice of witches, such as casting spells and performing magick.

From a Wiccan's perspective, Wicca is not particularly a religion, but a way of worshipping nature and living in balance with the Earth. It is symbolized by a pentacle, which is often placed on altars and points of worship.

In general, Wicca has been described as a fairly modern polytheistic pagan religious movement that stems from Western esoteric practices. Popularized by Gerald Gardner in the early 1950s, Wicca has grown over time in its principles and practices, including rituals, spells, and magic.

Although most scholars would prefer to regard it as a religion because it has objects of worship, there are many areas in which Wicca does not qualify as a religion. More so, Wiccans would rather focus on individual worship. This inevitably leads us to the next topic of discussion.

IS WICCA A RELIGION?

Maybe yes, and maybe not! As it continues to gain dominance over other pagan religions and practices, as well as acceptance, especially in the Western world, a lot of people have continued to question its nature, asking the question, is it a religion?

Most Wiccans, for a start, do not consider their practice a religion but view it as a form of spirituality and a way of life. Admittedly, this is a rather debatable topic that has continued to attract interest in scholarship. Judging by the fact that it has a connection with the supernatural and that it has objects of worship, one may describe Wicca as a religion.

But, on the other hand, there are certain facts about the practice that cause other scholars to argue that it is not a religion. A couple of them are discussed below.

NO DESIGNATED PLACE OF WORSHIP

Unlike many other religions — monotheistic or polytheistic —, Wicca does not have a particular place of worship. Islam and Christianity, for example, are characterized by the strict insistence on worshipping in the church and the mosque, respectively, and failure to adhere to this instruction is considered an aberration. In other words, worshipers must necessarily converge at such places of worship at the agreed time, but this is not the case with Wicca. Instead, worshipers are allowed the express freedom to conduct their worship in any public or private space they find comfortable. More so, there is no strict injunction that there has to be a group of people coming together at each point in time to worship. As a matter of fact, the emphasis is placed on individual worship.

NO RECOGNIZED BOOK OF WORSHIP

Again, Wicca differs from the major religions of the world with regards to a Holy book, or book of reference, or a guidebook or a book of conduct as the case may be. While Christianity, Islam, Buddhism and many other religions have a holy book or revered texts that guide their worship and conduct both with members of the same religion and with members of other religions, no such book is recognized in Wicca. In a way, this could be considered an advantage, as it does not confine members to a dogmatic belief in the words of a book. This is not to say, however, that Wicca is without its binding teachings, but that it is more liberal in its approach and that it emphasizes individuality over group affairs. In addition, it considers every individual capable of seeking and discovering their paths to the spirit realm all by themselves. On the contrary, the excessive individuality which Wicca is known for has brought about arbitrariness in its beliefs. Many divergent and conflicting practices and beliefs have resulted from different people under the umbrella of Wicca. A quick example is that while some Wiccans are pantheistic, who believe in the existence of a divine being in everything, most Wiccans are duotheistic, who believe in the existence of two divine beings (the Goddess and the God) which are not in conflict with each other but rather coexist. Wicca is essentially decentralized. It lacks a central structure of principles, beliefs and practices, and allows much freedom for individual worshippers to explore the spiritual path in their own way. The disadvantage of this is that it gives rise to disagreements in beliefs and practices among Wiccans. Although most Wiccans are duotheistic, smaller sects have emerged over time that are pantheistic and, in some other situations, monotheistic.

WHAT IS WITCHCRAFT? DO ALL WICCANS PRACTICE WITCHCRAFT?

Here is another vital question that has stemmed over the years from the confusing beliefs that Wiccans are witches (note the lower case 'w'). However, this confusion is not unfounded. To start with, both the words 'Wicca' and 'witch' originate from the same Anglo-Saxon word, which means 'the wise one'. More so, Gerald Gardner, a very important figure in the history of Wicca, largely referred to the religion as *the witch-cult, Craft of the wise,* and *Witchcraft*. The name 'Wicca' is believed to have been popularized later in the 1960s by British practitioners, key among whom was Charles Cardel. By modern description, witchcraft refers to the belief in and practices generally connected to rituals, spells, and magic with the aim to utilize cosmic powers for bringing about a desired effect or change in the physical world. Note that witchcraft is independent of religion. What this means is that an individual can choose to practice witchcraft without an association with any religion of the world. It also implies that witchcraft is not the stock-in-trade of Wiccans, even though they are otherwise called Witches. The term 'Witch' is a rather collective title by which all those who practice Wicca are called. By implication, practicing Wicca makes you a Witch, but being a witch does not make you a Wiccan since witchcraft is also associated with other pagan religions such as heathenry. Most Wiccans practice witchcraft, but this is not to say, however, that witchcraft is a compulsory practice in Wicca. Typical of the nature of Wicca, it allows room for individuals to exercise their choices and preferences, one of which is whether or not they want to connect to the metaphysical realm and utilize their psychic powers. Based on this, it is questionable to associate witchcraft with Wiccans only. More so, it is biased to view witchcraft in a negative light. The art involves spells, hexes, and curses on one hand, as well as benevolent and healing powers on the other hand. A witch's power comes by tapping into his/her personal internal abilities and from Nature as well as gods and spirits of the metaphysical realm, and these powers may be learned and acquired by personal efforts and studies, and not necessarily by a connection to Wicca or Amy other religion whatsoever.

IS WICCA CONNECTED TO SATANISM?

It seems to be necessary to preface every discussion of Witchcraft with an explanation that, no, Neo-Pagan Witches aren't Satanists.

Glory Zell

If this question has been bugging your mind, I'm afraid to disclose to you that the answer is neither yes nor no, but largely tends towards the latter. It is the major conception that all pagan religions worship or, at least, believe in the Devil. This is not the case for Wicca. To help you understand this clearly enough, a brief exposition to Satanism as a concept is necessary. Disciples of Satanism see Satan as their central figure of worship, although most new age Satanists do not consider Satan as a deity. Luciferians and Laveyans, institutionalized in the Church of Satan, are the main known Satanist groups. Other less common groups include agnostics, atheists, and apatheists, each with its own respective position. There is, however, nothing in the beliefs and practice system of Wicca that makes it Satanic in any way. First off, Wiccans do not worship Satan but believe in the duo of God and Goddess — I will walk you through the duotheistic nature of Wicca shortly. The Wiccan God and Goddess are very much unrelated to Satan in every way. Other than Satanists themselves, many other religious groups believe that Satan is an all-evil demonic entity with supernatural powers to cause mischief. This is especially the belief in Christianity, Islam and a few others. For Wiccans, Satan is completely nonexistent, let alone supernatural or evil.

THE WICCAN GOD AND GODDESS

Wicca is fundamentally built on the belief in and worship of two deities known simply as the Horned God and the Moon Goddess. The Goddess is believed to be the central deity of worship, with God as her consort. She is regarded as the trinity comprising the Maiden, Mother and the Crone. Wiccans hold that life originated from these two, even though the Goddess is primary. In some more modern versions of Wicca, however, the duo is equal in importance, and as a result, is revered equally. The Wiccan annual festivals, also addressed as the Wheel of the Year, revolve largely around the Goddess and the God, their courtship, the death of the God as well as His rebirth. It is to this duo that the Wiccan Rede, the most basic rule of behavior, which states that 'An [sic] it harm none, do what thou wilt' which, in modern language, translates as 'do whatever you like to do in as much as it portends no harm for anyone' holds its origin. Wiccans place so much value on festivals because they are the avenues for reestablishing the existence and essence of their Goddess and God. The festivals dedicated to God are, together, known as Sabbats, while those dedicated to the worship of the Goddess are called Esbats. These feasts correspond to the position of the Earth in relation to the Sun and the Moon respectively, hence they are worshipped at strategic periods of the year. They include the four cross-quarter days, the Equinoxes and several others. Based on this, if we may briefly revisit the question, is Wicca a religion, we would find that it passes as one because of the belief in gods and the practices. However, it should be mentioned that Wicca emphasizes individual discovery of supernatural forces and the ability to harness the benefits of the spirit over communal worship. This explains why there are hardly any covens and public places of worship.

INITIATION IN WICCA

For the benefit of those who might be digging into this book for the purpose of becoming a Wiccan or, put differently, a Witch, it is important to answer this significant question. How can you become a Witch? Does it require initiation? Can you initiate yourself? First off, it is the foundational belief in Wicca that the decision to become a Wiccan is entirely a product of personal choice. In other words, whoever became a Wiccan would have thought it through and decided by personal will and not by influence of any kind to become one. Moreover, it is impossible to become a Wiccan by inheritance. Even if your parent or relative is a Wiccan, you would necessarily have to decide to become a Wiccan. That said, it is important to note that becoming a Wiccan would require at least two stages, namely dedication and initiation. The first stage involves becoming familiar with Wiccan beliefs. This would require a committed study of the teachings and tenets of the Wiccan religion. This stage can be considered as the probationary period, as it determines whether they finally decide to become witches. It ranges from a period of a few days to a year, depending on the level of commitment and the period the individual personally requires to make up their mind. After the dedication stage and the individual has fully decided to become a

Wiccan, initiation follows. Initiation involves a formal rite that inducts the individual into the group. In most Wiccan practices, it involves a ceremony and minor rituals that require the potential Wiccan to, as in many other forms of initiation, swear their allegiance to the Wiccan path. Meanwhile, it is noteworthy that most modern Wiccan covens and groups have their specific initiation requirements, which the inductee is expected to fulfill before full initiation into the group. The requirements vary from group to group.

The questions that immediately follow this are, what about potential Wiccans who do not wish to belong to a coven? Does self-initiation count as valid? This topic has elicited divergent opinions among Wiccan practitioners and scholars. Whereas not all Wiccan groups approve of self-initiation, it is still in practice notwithstanding. Some groups hold that the roles of a superior Wiccan who can serve as a guide and instructor, particularly a High Priest or High Priestess, to the potential Wiccan cannot be replaced by the inductee's personal efforts. On the other hand, some Wiccan groups emphasize the individual personal initiation, establishing their position on the fact that the personal conviction and experience of the initiation process is all that is required to become a Witch.

This conflict in practice and belief remains unresolved to date among Wiccans. Either way, one unmistakable fact common to all Wiccan groups despite the existing differences is that the individual who wishes to become a Wiccan must be dedicated and committed to the faith. This does not, however, imply that one cannot partake in Wicca except one is initiated. As a matter of fact, you could participate in the open rituals and festivals if they interest you, whether or not you wish to become a member.

THE WICCAN SYMBOLS AND THEIR SIGNIFICANCE

A large number of symbols are unique to Wicca. Each of them has its historical foundation and significance, especially in the supernatural realm. Some of the most common ones are discussed in this section.

THE PENTACLE

The Pentacle is the most basic symbol of Wicca. It comprises a five-pointed star within a circle. The points, which point in different directions, symbolize the four classical elements of Earth, Air, Water and Fire, and the aether or Spirit. Together, these points represent balance and completeness.

However, the interpretation differs for some other Wiccan covens who hold that the five points symbolize the major distinct parts of the human body — the head, the arms, and the legs.Notwithstanding the different interpretations, you will most definitely find this signature symbol on every Wiccan altar you come across, whether personal or public.

THE TRIQUETRA AND THE TRISKELE

These symbols are joined as a complete piece. The three-pointed triangular knot is the triquetra, while the triskele are the spirals. Although these symbols originally belong to Celtic Christianity, over time they have become associated with Wicca. They represent the trinities and eternity, concepts very common in Christianity.

THE TRIPLE MOON

This is a rather common symbol of Wicca. It consists of a full moon at the center and a crescent on either side of it. This symbol is representative of the Wiccan Goddess — the Maiden, the Mother, and the Crone. It is also associated with birth, life, and death.

THE EIGHT-SPOKED WHEEL

The Wiccan annual festivals and celebrations are known as the Wheel, which comprises eight spokes. These festivals are known as Sabbats and, together, they make up the Wiccan calendar for a year. This wheel often has a somewhat red circle at the center, which represents the Sun.

THE SPIRAL GODDESS

The Wicca religion is essentially built on a Goddess. Despite the fact that it is duotheistic, involving the belief in two deities, the Goddess and the God, it tilts more heavily to the worship of the Goddess. More so, it is believed that the Goddess is the foundation of the life cycle of birth, life and death. This explains why so much value is placed on the Goddess. No wonder then that a special symbol is made to represent the Goddess. The Goddess is represented by a spiral image that shows a nude female with arms over her head. The spiral positioned in her midsection symbolizes her abilities to create and bring to life. The fact that it is nude is also symbolic. It represents the Goddess's fertility.

THE HORNED GOD

While the spiral Goddess represents the female deity, the Horned God is used to symbolize the masculinity and strength of the God. It is also representative of God's fertility and vegetation. Note that Wicca believes strongly in the reproductive essence of life. This cannot be achieved without a fertile God and a Goddess, which are believed to be the origin of life and being.

THE ORIGINS OF WICCA

What is today known as Wicca has, no doubt, undergone a series of evolutionary processes over the years with some religious borrowings and additions here and there. In addition, several subsets have developed over time. This makes it an interesting cause, therefore, to undertake a brief historical study of the religion.

Wicca owes its roots to the teachings of the Englishman Gerald Brousseau Gardner, who lived from 1884 to 1964 and spent most of his retirement period in Asia, by virtue of which he was exposed to many ancient occult practices. A few years before the outbreak of WW II, he returned to England and founded the modern Wicca based on the worship of a female deity, respect for nature and practice of magick. Within this period, Gardner gathered a number of disciples, significant among whom was Doreen Valiente, with whom he wrote and published several books that emphasized the esoteric nature and practices of the movement. One such book is *Witchcraft Today*, published in 1954.

Gardner's disciples were initiated into covens, and the practice grew rapidly in the Western world, albeit with various slight alterations from what it was at the beginning. By 1980, there were some 15,000 Wiccans in Western Europe and the North American regions. However, it was met with severe criticism. Later in the century, a different particular version of Wicca known as Dianic Wicca, led by one Alexander Sander who perceived the religion as a religion of women and therefore worshipped only the Goddess. Another major difference that characterized this version of Wicca was that they refused to be called Witches.

Wicca spread to the United States in the late 1960s with much emphasis placed on nature as well as unconventional lifestyles and search for spirituality in contrast to the earlier traditional religions. Covens comprised mainly of about 10 to 15 members who became members by initiation. They could then grow from mere coven members to the priesthood after mastering the art of magic and were conversant with the Wiccan rituals.

Despite the fact that when it started in the 20th century, it set out as a single practice with a unified body of ancient pagan practices and rituals and beliefs with the same theological structure, Wicca has diversified a lot in the present age. This explains why it does not have a central figure of authority or a centralized organization. Its basic beliefs and structure have undergone many variations. Similarly, its sects, traditions and lineages have become largely decentralized, to the point that scholars have concluded that there is hardly a single sect or version of modern Wicca that accurately represents what the movement was in the 19th century. As a matter of fact, the disagreement in structure and beliefs remain unresolved to date. At the moment, there are thousands of Wiccan groups spread across the English-speaking world and Northern and Western Europe loosely coordinated by two recognized international groups known as The Pagan Federation and the Universal Federation of Pagans. No doubt, Wicca has undergone a series of changes, modifications, and readaptations over time, but notwithstanding, there are certain beliefs and practices which are common to all the contemporary neopagan Wiccan groups.

CHAPTER SUMMARY

This chapter discusses the most basic questions about Wicca — the meaning, history, and forms of Wicca. It ushers you into the details of the neopagan religion, the Wiccan God and Goddess and other associated deities. It also walks you through the process of initiation into the Wiccan religion as well as its demands and sacrifices.

CHAPTER TWO.

THE BASIC PRINCIPLES AND PRACTICES OF WICCA

WHAT THEY BELIEVE, DO AND TEACH

It is no exaggeration that if you ask five or ten Wiccans about Wicca, you are bound to have completely different responses or at least minor variations. The reasons for this aren't farfetched: there is no Wiccan guidebook or Holy book, and there is no strict regulatory body to curb the growing differences. More so, Wicca emphasizes individuality over group worship. This, therefore, underscores its esoteric nature and the growing diversification to which it is continually subjected. Based on this, there are many conflicting beliefs and practices plaguing Wicca as a neopagan religion. The consequence of this is double-sided. While diversification makes Wicca an interesting topic of research and discourse, it also makes the differences difficult to reconcile, and this has slowed down its acceptance among non-Wiccans. Based on this, the focus of this chapter will rest mainly on the beliefs and practices common to most Wiccan covens.

THE SOVEREIGNTY OF THE GODDESS AND THE GOD

Every Wiccan group is founded on the belief in the existence and sovereignty of the Moon Goddess. Although not all covens are duotheistic, almost all of them believe in the existence of the Goddess and her male counterpart. Both deities are believed to be responsible for life and fertility. Special days of the year are designated for the

162

worship of the Goddess and the God respectively. These are the Wiccan holidays which, collectively, are known as the Wheel of the Year. In a subsequent part of this book, I dedicate a full chapter to the discussion of each of these festivals, as well as their significance for a Wiccan.

In addition to the Goddess and God, Wiccans believe in other deities, which are considered smaller in authority and honor. These are referred to as the deities of the respective Wiccan traditions. Some of them are Cerridwen, Herne, Apollo, Athena, Isis, and so on. In most covens, the particular small deity of worship is known only to the coven members. Whatever the small deity of worship is, one fact remains unmistakable about Wiccan groups. They all believe in the power of the divine, hence they emphasize the need to personally attain the state of constant connection to the supernatural.

ONLY INITIATES ARE ALLOWED IN THE DEEP CIRCLES

To be upfront enough, Wicca is not discriminatory, but it draws the lines between initiates and non-initiates. As much as it allows nonmembers ample room to be partakers of public festivals and minor activities, it doesn't allow them access to the core rituals of the group.

For example, the particular small deity which a particular coven believes in is revealed to its initiates only. Wicca is occultic in nature and therefore values initiation. Initiation often involves a thorough process but must begin with the potential Wiccans, making up their minds to be a member. This stage is never forced or hurried. The covens allow such persons access to minor practices and public festivals for a period of time in order to help them decide whether or not they would really love to be part. Once this stage has been completed and the decision to join has been made, the first initiation follows.

The first initiation is a rebirth of the individual, the process of which initiates dedicate themselves to the cause and activities of the group in order to show themselves as worthy members. Upon successfully completing the first stage, they are made to undergo the second initiation. After becoming a full member, a Wiccan can study and practice well enough to progress through the ranks otherwise known as degrees. Only those who have reached the Third Degree are capable enough to become High Priestesses or Priests. Self-initiation is only allowed for those who wish to practice Wicca in solitary.

MAGIC IS A TOOL FOR SELF-EXPRESSION

Magic, sometimes alternately spelled 'magick', is another basic practice in Wicca. It is interesting to mention that Wiccans do not consider magic as a supernatural ability, but merely as a set of spells with which an individual harnesses his inner forces to redirect the natural energy around him to suit his intentions. This requires spells, crystals, wand, candles, study and the likes. Magic appears to be literally practiced in Wicca. In other words, any Wiccan can engage in magic in as much as they possess the skills required, but there are certain regulations that bind its practice. First off, magic is only practiced within a sacred circle, and rules such as the Law of Threefold Return, which is also known as the Rule of Three, and the Wiccan Rede are to prevent Wiccans from using their magical powers to the detriment of others.

These rules, however, are part of the efforts to differentiate the Wiccan practice of magic from the sometimes harmful magic practiced by other groups. Wiccan magic is often done during rituals as a group and could also be individually practiced. In a later part of this book, I discuss the significance of magic to Wiccans and how you could harness your magical powers.

THE SPIRIT WORLD IS REAL

The reality of the supernatural world is emphasized in Wiccan practice. Literally, all Wiccan groups believe that there exists a metaphysical world with which we can interact. This involves communication with the dead, with certain spirits and sometimes with powerful demons who serve as spirit guides. Communication with such metaphysical powers is made possible via a series of methods, including astrology, tarots, and runes. This also relates strongly to the belief in ancestry. It is the belief in Wicca that those who are long dead are actively watching over the living. In other words, the ancestors are powerful enough to oversee, protect and influence the lives and activities of those living. This, according to Wiccans, makes it a necessity to constantly commune with the ancestors.

THERE IS LIFE AFTER NOW

One of the guiding principles of Wicca is that there is life after death and that whatever one does in the present life comes back to influence one's experience in the next one. This principle is not to be mistaken with the Christian and Islamic belief in Heaven, Hell, eternity and sin. On the contrary, Wicca does not believe in such concepts. Rather, it emphasizes that life continues afterlife. Put differently, after the current life, there is another life. It also emphasizes that karma is real and that whatever one does now, whether good or otherwise, will be revisited on one later on. This payback principle is enshrined in the Law of Threefold Return. It is in order to enjoy a peaceful and fruitful afterlife that Wicca preaches harmlessness. The Wiccan Rede is a summary of this belief: harm no one. As a result of this, everyone must be willing to accept responsibility for their actions and inactions. Whatever the consequences of your acts are, whether positive or otherwise, Wiccans believe that you must be willing to take responsibility for such actions.

THE DIVINE IS PRESENT IN NATURE

There is a pantheistic connotation in this Wiccan principle. Most, if not all, Wiccan groups believe that the Divine is present in every natural thing. They hold that although the Goddess and God are supreme deities, they manifest in humans, animals, plants, insects, and every other natural thing in the environment. Hence, they revere every natural element, believing that every natural element is sacred since the Divine is present in them. This reinforces the reason why they emphasize the possibility of communicating with supernatural beings. They maintain that everyone, regardless of rank, can communicate with the Divine and not only priests.

FESTIVALS ARE BASED ON NATURE

To further buttress the value which Wicca places on nature, it must be mentioned that all Wiccan festivals and celebrations are based on the rotation of the earth in relation to the Sun. Based on the resulting seasons, Wicca holds eight major annual celebrations, which are known as Sabbats, as well as other monthly festivals called Esbats. You will find a more detailed discussion of the respective festivals in a subsequent chapter in this book.

RESPECT AND TOLERANCE OF OTHER RELIGIONS

It is a rare phenomenon to find Wiccans in altercations with individuals of other faiths based on beliefs. The major secret behind this is the Wiccan tolerance for other faiths. More so, they do not proselytize their practices or preach to others to become part of their faith. This is because they believe in the personal journey to spiritual discovery. An individual who becomes a Wiccan will do so out of personal conviction and not through any kind of influence or inheritance.The beliefs and practices of Wicca are definitely inexhaustible, owing to the diversification that has rocked it over the years. Based on this, it is almost impossible for even Wiccans and scholars of Wicca to agree on a comprehensive body of beliefs and guide system that binds all Wiccan groups. Some common examples of diversification are whether Wicca is monotheistic or duotheistic and whether self-initiation is allowed or not. These differences, among others, remain unresolved and explain the slow acceptance of the faith. This situation, notwithstanding, does not completely mean that there are no common grounds whatsoever in Wicca. On the contrary, there are a number of them. Some of the most common areas of concord are discussed above, and it is my belief that they give you a detailed understanding of the neopagan Wiccan faith. More revelations to follow in the subsequent chapters.

CHAPTER SUMMARY

In this chapter, you will find the fundamental beliefs and principles that form the pillars and foundation of Wicca as a religion, as well as how they apply to you as a beginner Witch.

CHAPTER THREE.

WICCA AND MAGIC

HOW TO HARNESS YOUR PERSONAL MAGICAL POWERS

Many believe magic to be simply another law of nature, albeit one that is poorly understood and written off as fakery.

Wesley Baines

The topic of magic often sparks both interest and controversy in the field of Wicca. It is common to find people develop an interest in becoming Witches solely because of the magic involved in Wicca. In the same vein, some others are interested in discovering the supposed supernaturality behind the performance of magic. Hence, several questions have cropped up, including the following:

- What exactly is the Wiccan Magic?

- Is Magic any different from Magick?

- What is Black magic?

- What is White Magic?

- Who are those allowed to practice magic?

- Is Magic associated with Wicca?

- Do all Wiccans practice Magic?

- What does it require to practice magic?

- Is Magic necessarily evil?

On and on that way, the questions run in numbers. Although I have hinted at the topic earlier, it is my focus in this chapter to unveil the truths about Wicca and Magic in full. The term 'Magic' describes the process and practice of manipulating natural forces using one's personal powers and will to bring about desired changes in the universe. It is often the case that such changes cause awe, especially among those not skilled in the art. This is achievable through a variety of methods, including spellcasting, rituals, candles, making potions, dances, incantations, wands, and so on. Magic as a concept is quite broader than Wicca. By this, I mean, magic is not an exclusive practice of Wiccans. Individuals and groups who are not in any way related to Wicca have always practiced and still practice magic. This implies that although magic is an essential part of Wicca, it is not an exclusive practice of the neopagan religion. However, it must be mentioned that the term 'Magick' did not exist until the 19th century. The alteration was introduced and popularized via the works of Aleister Crowley, a key figure in the British Wiccan movement in the 19th and 20th centuries. This alteration was to establish a difference between Wiccan magic and the activities of illusionists and stage magicians, whose trade was to entertain people with their magical powers. What is known today as magic exclusively describes the revered activities of Wiccans and is also referred to as witchcraft or simply "The Craft". To a large extent, Wiccan magic is not very different in form from known ancient magic, as it involves the same process and practice of bringing about changes in the physical realm with the aid of supernatural powers. However, the goal is different.

WHY THE WICCAN MAGICK?

Admittedly, people perform magic for diverse purposes ranging from personal to commercial purposes. One could do magic to land themselves a better job, to avert dangers or protect themselves from harm, to get a partner, to recover from an ailment, to get wealthier, and a host of several other personal reasons. For Wiccans, however, the aim is not entirely so personal. This is not to say that Wiccans do not use magic for personal gain, protection and so on, but rather, they see magic as a more spiritual journey for a Wiccan to express themselves. This explains why magick is a core part of the Wiccan festivals and rituals. At each of the Wheel of the Year festivals (Sabbats and Esbats), magic is incorporated into the activities. They also perform spellwork on a large scale at the New Moon celebrations. On such occasions, in addition to the magic tools employed, they call upon the Goddess and the God, as well as the smaller deities, to manifest their heart desires.

THE CONTROVERSY OF MAGICK: SUPERNATURAL OR PHYSICAL?

Here is one of the most technical and unresolved long-standing debates revolving around Wicca. Even among Wiccans, it has been difficult to agree on the cosmic nature of Magick. Is it supernatural or physical? Although the practice of Magick is unanimous among

Wiccans, they have yet to agree on its nature. Several scholars have, over the years, contributed their thoughts and opinions to this debate. For Aleister Crowley and Wesley Baines, Magick is rather natural, controlled by the human will. Hence, he defined it as "the science and art of causing change to occur in conformity with Will." Although his definition of magick may be criticized for being rather too broad, his position that it is completely physical is unmistakable. Wesley Baines is much more assertive in his position when he noted that "Many believe magic to be simply another law of nature, albeit one that is poorly understood and written off as fakery. As such, magic is not supernatural, but just as natural as gravity and wind, and often involves a combination of invocations, movement, music, meditation, and tools." Based on this, magic is considered a purely natural phenomenon in which the forces of nature are controlled by super (not supernatural) powers and the human will. Some go as far as reducing it to the control of the five senses. In a way, this might appear to be the case, but one fact that cannot be rubbed off is that you cannot practice magic, or in essence, control the forces of nature, simply by sheer will or by wishing it into existence but through series of processes, incantations, and spells which are in no way ordinary. This position contradicts the view of the scholars mentioned above and is backed by the fact that not all Wiccans can perform magick even though they believe in its reality.

BLACK MAGIC VS WHITE MAGIC

Questions revolving around types of magic are often raised by non-Wiccans, and this is understandable due to the existing stereotypical dichotomy between black and white and the association of these colors with good and evil respectively. It is based on such a mindset that people ask questions such as; Is White Magick good? Is Black Magick necessarily evil? Is a Wiccan allowed to practice Black Magick?

To start with, many Wiccans who described their own magic as white did it with the unfair belief that there is another magical practice that is black. More so, they associated 'White' with good, pleasant and favorable, and therefore used it to describe their version of Wiccan magick, which supposedly involves no harm to others, is used to improve their own living conditions, protect themselves from harm, among other 'good intentions'. This classification began with Helena Blavatsky in the 19th century. Early notable Wiccan leaders such as Sybil Leek, Alex Winfield, and Alex Sanders also belonged to this school of thought. However, many modern Wiccans have come to criticize this dichotomy. It is questionable to assume that 'Black Magick' essentially means wicked practices or is related to evil and Satanism. This is buttressed by the fact that there is nothing in the semantic make-up of 'Black' to warrant its association with evil. More so, Satanism has grown from the ancient association with the Devil. This is true to the extent that modern Satanist groups such as Luciferians and LaVeyan Satanists do not acknowledge that Satan is evil. Why then should 'black magick' be regarded as evil?

HARM TO NONE: THE GUIDING RULE

A most vital guiding principle to the practice of magic in Wicca is what is summarized as the Wiccan Rede, which is believed to have been formulated by Priestess Doreen Valiente in the 20th century. The Wiccan Rede reads thus: *"An' it harm none, do what ye will."* In everyday language, it means to do what you will in as much as it harms no one. By implication, no one is allowed to discomfit, let alone deliberately harm, others by their practice of magick. In other words, all magicks should be positively geared toward improving one's life as well as those of others around. The rule is a binding one that goes beyond the practice of magic. It is basically the Wiccan's daily watchword. As it is the case that virtually every Wiccan who chooses to is allowed to practice magick, irrespective of the rank or coven, the Rede forms an essential way of checkmating excesses and abuse.

HARNESSING YOUR MAGICAL POWERS

It is undeniable that many people become Witches solely or initially for the purpose of using magic to enhance their lives in one way or the other. My focus, for now, is not on whether this is a justifiable cause or the foundational cause for becoming a Wiccan or not. For whatever reason you wish to become a Wiccan, if the practice of magic interests you, this section is directed at you to make your journey into the practice of magic much easier, fun and productive. There are various methods of magical practices among which candle magic, crystal magic and herbal magic will form our major concern at this time.

CANDLE MAGIC

Candle magic is perfect as a starting point for beginners in magic. Its effectiveness is based on the energies of fire and flame, which humans have long used for different purposes, both secular and supernatural, since the beginning of time. To begin with, fire was fundamental to the existence of early man. It was a source of illumination, in addition to the natural duo of the Sun and the Moon. It was also a way of supplicating and invoking the spirit of the ancestors to bring the desires of the human heart into physical reality. This line of thought has transcended the ancient world, where fire, in the form of fireballs and candles, was used for illumination. It remains significant even in the modern world, where more sophisticated lighting has been invented. The most common and perhaps the most significant is the practice of blowing out candles after making wishes during birthday celebrations. In a way, it is an indirect recognition of the ability of fire to make the heart's desires come true. A candle is symbolic and representative of the elements. The base of the candle, for example, represents the element Earth, which helps keep the flame lit and rooted. Wax, on the other hand, undergoes a process of transformation from solid to liquid to gaseous state, a phenomenon that is representative of the Water element. Along the same lines, the Air element is incorporated into the process, since oxygen is necessary to light the fire and keep it burning, while the flame itself is symbolic of the Fire element. The fifth element — Spirit — comes to play in the wishes and desires that you speak unto the candle. Candle seems to embody the entire universe and its energies, hence it is said to be very effective. More so, the flames of the candle are able to conjure up the required atmosphere for one to connect with the forces in the universe and to bring about the desired effect in the physical realm. Depending on the purpose of the magic and some other factors put in place, such as the spells, magic could make you feel powerful, peaceful and connected. There is also the dimension of color in candle magic. Depending on the purpose of the magical practices, you might want to enforce it with colors. Bear in mind that colors have specific spiritual connotations and should, therefore, not be mismatched. Colors such as red, white, green, purple, black and a few others are known for their significance. Red, for example, is associated with love, passion, and emotions; Purple with royalty and wealth; White with cleanliness and purity; black with death and gloom, and green with growth, abundance, and life. Combining color with candle magic alongside spells and other items is believed to be much more effective in candle magic. As the candle burns out and the shape disappears, or rather, melts into wax, it is assumed that the desires which it bears are conveyed via the flames to the ethereal world where it is transformed into reality that comes back to manifest in the physical world. Provided below is an extensive list of possible candle colors you could use and a few tips to guide you in your candle selection and use:

- Red: Courage and health, sexual love, and lust

- Pink: Friendship, affection, and love

- Orange: Attraction and encouragement

- Gold: Financial gain and business endeavors

- Yellow: Persuasion and protection

- Green: Financial wealth, abundance, and fertility

- Light Blue: Health, patience, and understanding

- Dark Blue: Depression and vulnerability

- Brown: Earth-related or animal-related workings

- Black: Negativity and banishment

- Purple: Ambition, royalty, and power

- Silver: Reflection and intuition

- White: Purity and truth

Note the following simple tips as you select and apply your candle magic:

- In the absence of the wanted colors, you could use a white candle for whatever purpose.

- Never use the same candle twice. This is because candles are capable of receiving vibrations and could elicit negative results as a result.

- Special candles such as short taper candles or votive candles are the best.

- Accompany your candle magic with short incantations or mantras, declaring your desires into reality. You could choose to repeat this silently as you gaze at the candle.

- On the other hand, you can write it on a small piece of paper, fold it neatly and put it in the candle container to burn.

- Focus on your intentions and not just on the burning flames.

- Dispose of the candle wax after the process.

- On the other hand, if you wish to read answers to your requests immediately, simply drop the wax into a bowl of water. It will instantly solidify into shapes. The shapes will form the answers you seek.

HERBAL MAGIC

Wiccans place as much value on herbal magick as they do on candle magick, although the former may be a bit more demanding. Herbal magick was practiced long before Wicca arose. Its origin goes back to the beginning of time because plants and herbs in their many species were available to early peoples for both consumption and therapeutic purposes. Back then, the healing of physical ailments was accompanied by small rituals and prayers that were believed to promote the efficacy of the herbal concoction. To this day, people continue to enjoy the therapeutic powers of herbs and shrubs through daily tea and coffee, as well as herbal beverages. Undoubtedly, these herbal drinks are magical in their own way.

Like candle magic, herbal magic incorporates the four basic elements of nature: wind, fire, air and earth, which contribute to its effectiveness. Plant seeds are buried in the earth, where they first decompose and come back to life after receiving the action of certain minerals in the soil. The soil also serves as a perpetual source of nutrients for the plants as they grow. This is closely contributed to by the Water element present in the soils or added manually. But this is not enough. Plants need to interact with the Fire element through sunlight, otherwise growth is impossible. It is after this that the exchange of carbon dioxide and oxygen becomes possible, a process involving the Air element. In addition to the four basic elements discussed, scholars have argued that plants also possess the Spirit element, and this is arguably so.

Aristotle, for a start, argued that plants possess a level of intelligence, which he described as 'psyches' by which he meant the quality of having a soul and spirit. This assertion has grown into a belief among Wiccans today, who hold that plants are entities of their own with a spirit, hence their (Wiccans) reverence of nature. Lots of plant scientists have, over time, backed up Aristotle's claims, asserting that plants have consciousness, a quality that makes them aware of the nature of their environment, the other plants around, insects as well as animals. They also possess enough intelligence to react adequately to the insects and animals around them. This cooperation is natural and made possible via an underground network of roots as well as chemicals released into the air to warn other plants of a predatory attack, especially from insects. These scientific discoveries are proof of the Ethereal dimension of plants and, by extension, herbal magic. The harmonious interaction of these elements strengthens herbal magic, giving it all the effectiveness needed to bring about the change desired by its users. What Wiccans do when using seeds, stems, flowers, barks, roots and berries in their herbal magick is to harness the natural energies of plants. Whether inside or outside of Wicca, herbs are used in a variety of ways. For example, they can be used with candle magic.

Smudging, which consists of burning dried herbs to purify the environment, is also a common practice even among Wiccans. Herbal magic is used in rituals, and there are special herbs exclusively used in the Sabbat rituals. If you are new to herbal magic, rest assured that you do not have to become a botanist or a master gardener before you can effectively utilize the herbs. It is true that you do not necessarily need to master all the magical properties of all the herbs that there are at a time. Rather, you should take it one herb at a time, making sure to understand the features and specific application of that particular herb before using it. This is necessary to avoid misuse. Herbs such as henbane and belladonna could be highly toxic and deadly. Below is a list of common herbs used in Wicca and their uses and application:

ROSEMARY

One of the known ancient herbs, Rosemary has always been used for promoting love in an atmosphere where it is needed by warding off negative energy.

But beyond that, it also helps to strengthen the human brain, aids reasoning and remembrance, as well as protects from evil spirits. You can choose to burn it while meditating to keep your arena safe from negative vibes.

Modern Wiccans now also use Rosemary to protect their homes from burglars. Simply hang it at your doorpost.

MUGWORT

Mugwort is a trusted herb for increasing productivity and also for mental abilities. It is highly versatile, can be grown in any environment. It can also be used in diverse situations, ranging from smudging to spellwork to incense. If you would like to use mugwort to bring productivity at your workplace of fertility in your home, all you have to do is burn it in the arena or smudge it during divination rituals. Mugwort is, however, forbidden to be touched by pregnant women.

CHAMOMILE

This beautiful herb helps to relieve stress, brings luck and is also used for purification purposes. If you have difficulty sleeping, focusing on your meditation or relaxing, simply sprinkle it around your home. You could also employ it to protect against evil or magical attacks. For gamblers, chamomile brings good luck. You can wear it as a garland around your neck or, if you are not so daring, just carry a few of them in your pocket, and that's it!

LAVENDER

Like chamomile, lavender brings about relief and calmness. But one important purpose people use lavender for is love. If you have problems with hatred or you suffer too much rejection from people, you need love, and lavender does the magic for you. Carry it around with you everywhere you go or hang it in your home. If you are mentally troubled or you find it difficult to sleep, stuff a few lavender pieces underneath your pillow before going to bed, and you're bound to get a peaceful sleep.

SAGE

Sage is useful for various magical goals. For generations, people have used sage for purifying their homes and environment and also for cleansing, especially during rituals. This is done by burning dry sage twigs.

However, it has been adopted for more uses than that. Inhaling the smoke is believed to sharpen one's mind and increase one's wisdom. In addition, sage could bring your wishes to reality.

This is done by writing wishes on a sage leaf and leaving the leaf under the pillow. It is believed that if you dream of your wish in the next three to five days, your wish will come true.

YARROW

If you often lose courage or develop heavy feet when it is time to make valid decisions or take important steps, you definitely lack courage, and this is the right herb for you.

All you need to do is to wear it on you when you need the confidence to carry out something important. It magically subdues your low self-esteem, overcomes your fears and boosts your confidence level.

Also known as Knight's Milfoil or Woundwort, yarrow is useful for treating injuries too. Some Wiccan groups use it for boosting passionate love in marriage. Simply hang it over your bed!

Other common herbs that are predominantly used in Wicca are Bay leaf, Dandelion, Basil, Hibiscus, Cinnamon, Star Anise, Thyme, Nutmeg, Elecampane, Valerian, among others.

CRYSTAL MAGIC

The third method of magic, which is as well worthy of mention, is crystal magic. If you already know about crystals, it wouldn't amaze you too much to learn that they are also used by Witches for rituals and for magic in general. Crystals, also known as stones, refer to a wide variety of solid minerals that have various shapes and colors and can be organic or inorganic. Crystals operate on vibrations and colors and are believed to have healing powers. It is, therefore, no wonder that they are precious items to Wiccans. Although true crystals such as Clear Quartz, Amethyst and Rose Quartz have been found to emit more vibrations and charges, and, as a result, perform better in Wiccan magic than the processed ones such as jade and bloodstone, among others, which are made from an artificial combination of two or more minerals, Wiccans use all crystals alike but with a full understanding of their respective compositions and magical abilities. Like candles and herbs, crystals are also representative of the five elements — Fire, Air, Wind, Water, and Spirit. Wiccans believe that crystals are alive, and this belief is not without basis. To start with, if you hold a crystal in your hand, you will testify to the fact that it emits some natural energy and has an effect on you. Experts have described this as the piezoelectric effect. More so, if you happen to hit a crystal softly with an iron substance or squeeze it in your hands, you will notice that it releases an electric charge. It is the subtle energy inherent in crystals that Wiccans explore to drive their wishes and make them into reality, and also to bring about real change in the physical realm. To be a little more detailed, crystals are used in Wicca for a variety of purposes. It is common to use crystals to mark the circle on the floor before commencing rituals. Beyond this, however, each crystal has a specific use to which it is put, ranging from divination to healing to protection to meditation, and so on. In addition, crystals are used with the other magic methods — candle magic and herbal magic — and spells. In the next few paragraphs, you will find a list of the most commonly used crystals as well as their functions and how to rightly apply them in order to guide you in selecting yours:

AGATE

Agate is one of the most essential stones in crystal magic. Especially useful for casting spells, it helps to restore all lost energy and could also be useful for therapeutic purposes. It provides a relaxing experience, sporadically increases creativity and intellectual abilities, hence it is used for children and teenagers, who are still in their developmental stage. It is connected to the earth element, and as a result, makes you feel safe and grounded. This explains why it is used in spells meant for protection too.

AMETHYST

To start with, Amethyst is useful for scrying into the future because it helps to clear one's psyche, sharpen the intuition and enhance one's ability to focus. This explains why most Wiccans or members of other Pagan religions who prophesy or read the future prefer to use it in their practice. More so, it is a stone known to alleviate sicknesses, especially mental ailments. It also helps reduce addictions, check dangerous and detrimental behaviors, as well as eliminate the effects of alcohol. During rituals and festivals, Wiccans use it to clear the arena.

CITRINE

Here is one stone everyone who believes in the power of crystals should have. It helps in many great ways. If you have problems with expressing yourself convincingly or you suffer an inferiority complex or lack of confidence, you should consider keeping this stone within reach. It provides you with the needed confidence to communicate effectively with others in the family, at social circles and at work. It also clears off negative energy and keeps your day bright and positive all along.

MOONSTONE

This white, or sometimes pale blue, the stone helps to strengthen one's self-awareness and positive understanding of self. Although it is often associated with females, it is equally useful to male users. It boosts the confidence level and increases creativity as well.

GREEN JADE

There is quite a number of jade types, but the green jade stands out among all for its amazing ability to heal emotional imbalance. It is considered a dream stone because it grants access to the spirit world and gives insight into rituals. Jade bestows long life on its possessor and aids early recovery from infirmities. It is a stone of friendship and good luck.

It promotes love and both interpersonal and intrapersonal understanding. It gives wisdom and clarity, improves your emotional state, and strengthens the power of love. It also dispels negative energies.

QUARTZ

Like Jade, there are various forms of Quartz as well, but the most vital ones to Wiccans are Clear Quartz and Rose Quartz. Clear Quartz is a pure stone that helps to clear the mind. More so, it amplifies energy, boosts memory and causes heightened consciousness. Clear Quartz is helpful for logical reasoning and effective communication. It also helps to prepare the environment for meditation by warding off negative spirits that could cause distraction. Rose Quartz, on the other hand, gives you the inner energy you need to outgrow your fears. It brings you peace, satisfaction and makes you fall in love completely with yourself. More so, it strengthens the relationship between groups, family and friends. The list of crystals used in Wicca is inexhaustive. It is advisable to start with one stone at a time, depending on what your magical goals are. If you are not sure how to apply the crystals, note that different crystals have their respective ways of using them. Whereas you need to put some underneath your pillow or bed, some of them are meant to be carried about, and on and on. I provide below a few random tips to guide you through crystal magic:

- You could carry crystals such as Clear Quartz, Jade and citrine with you. Leave them in your bag, pockets, or anything you're carrying. You could also wear them as necklaces if the occasion permits such. They will give you the confidence to face the day's challenges, protect you from negative forces, help you to stay focused and goal-oriented all day long!

- Sleeping with crystals under your pillow or bed is another way of using the stones as a form of magic. If you are suffering from insomnia or fitful nights, or you need a dream revelation, leaving stones such as selenite, jasper, and amethyst under your pillow is a dependable approach.

- Place the crystal(s) on your desires. This would require you to write out your wishes on a piece of paper, or better still, a wish book strictly for the purpose, and select the right stone that would achieve the wish you want at that point in time. Leave the wish list and the crystal in a warm corner of your home or office as the case may be, but be sure it is not a point where it would be disturbed. You should revisit the list from time to time or change the stone depending on the goals.

- Crystals can also be used with the other methods of Wiccan magic. What matters is that you align the goal of the candle magic or herbal magic with the particular stone in use. Put differently, ensure that the stone you are using is meant to achieve the same purpose as the other method.

- Never fail to cleanse your stones! Crystals attract negative energies a lot because of the vibrations. When the charge is used up, they could become useless and detrimental to your purpose. This makes it necessary to cleanse your stones before and after each use. There are many different ways to clear crystals, but the least demanding is to leave them outside under the sun for some period of time.

The subject of magic in Wicca is quite interesting and inexhaustible. You will be interested to know that, despite all that I have revealed in this chapter, I have only scratched the surface of the subject. This is to say that the Wiccan magic is a broad and multifaceted discourse that could take volumes upon volumes to walk through. Notwithstanding, you must bear in mind that there is always a starting point, and this will definitely form a good guide as you begin.

The most vital thing to note as you embark on your journey into the Wiccan magic is that irrespective of what magic method you use, the ultimate power to bring about the wanted change rests in your spirit.

Call upon the Goddess and God to protect you and teach you the secrets of magic. Ask stones and plants to reveal their powers - and listen.

Scott Cunningham

CHAPTER SUMMARY

Chapter three is centered on the Wiccan magick and its significance in the life of a Witch. If you are looking to become a Wiccan so as to develop magical powers, you will find all the answers to your questions carefully layered in this chapter. It discusses all the major magick types in Wicca — Candle magic, Crystal magic, and Herbal magic — without failing to guide you through the practice.

CHAPTER FOUR.

THE FIVE ELEMENTS AND WICCA

UNDERSTANDING THE ROLES OF THE NATURAL ELEMENTS

The five elements play a central role in all Wiccan activities. In many neo-pagan religions and spiritual traditions, the classical elements are usually referred to as elements are Earth, Fire, Air, Water and a fifth element called Spirit. In most cases, when the elements are mentioned, they are usually four, but there is another more elusive element that is difficult to describe and this element is usually called either Ether or Spirit. Spirit is the most ethereal of all the Wiccan elements and is usually regarded as a mystical and magical force that cannot be fathomed. When spell casting or practicing magic, you are considered to be working with the symbolism and characteristics corresponding to each of the elemental energies. The spirit element is sometimes also called Akasha, and each of these elements is represented in the pentagram. According to Wiccan beliefs, these elements serve as fundamental building blocks of the universe and are found in everything across the world. They believe that these elements are responsible for the eternal cycle of destruction as well as creation at the heart of all life, as well as universal existence. These elements pose as the literal forces of nature, and so they are sacred and revered by the Wiccans. All of these elements are in one way or the other incorporated into ritual and magic and ultimately, it is also incorporated into the daily consciousness of people who live with the natural rhythms of life, death, and rebirth – the cycle of existence. Every aspect and element of material existence is bound up in air, fire, earth, and water, while the fifth element, the spirit, is present in all

190

other elements. The timeless philosophy about the concept of the elemental states of matter has been since the time of the ancient Greeks, when what we now call the four classical elements were discussed by the great philosophers. These four substances – Air, Earth, Fire, and Water are believed to be the building blocks of all existing matter in the sense that nothing physical existed without being composed of one or more of them. They are said to make up all of the matter.

This worldview of the elements informed the medical practices of the ancient Greek society, as well as most of their spiritual traditions and ultimately, the elemental paradigm, came to influence the discovery of the physical elements of contemporary chemistry today. The Greeks were not the only ones to grasp the concept that all material existence arose from a handful of natural phenomena. The Egyptians in ancient Egypt and the Babylonians also hold some of these concepts, including Hinduism, Buddhism and the religions generally associated with the Chinese and Japanese people. Some of the Eastern traditions have a different recognition of these elements, such as Chinese astrology. Chinese astrologers distinguish earth-based substances of wood and metal as individual elements, while ancient Indian philosophy relates to the original Greek system but added **Akasha,** also referred to as space, as their fifth element. This Indian philosophy of a fifth element, Akasha was later borrowed by western occultists and is used in some Wiccan traditions to refer to *Spirit.*

THE CLASSICAL ELEMENTS

The classical elements are believed to be distinct spiritual energies and serve as an essential part of the Wiccan ritual. They are usually invoked at the start of a ritual to participate in the celebration at hand and in the performance of magic. Each of these elements is associated with the four cardinal directions – North, East, West, and South. The elements are typically called upon by the ritual celebrant, who then turns to face each direction to address as well as invite the spirit of the element into the circle. This act is called *calling the quarters* in many Wiccan traditions, while others simply refer to the act as invoking the elements. These elemental energies are then dismissed at the end of the ritual before the circle is closed.

Each of the classical elements is represented by one or more ritual tools on the Wiccan altar-like Earth, for instance. The pentacle symbolizes Earth, while a designated candle symbolizes Fire, a full or empty chalice symbolizes Water and a wand can be used as a symbol for Air. There may be other tools or instruments to symbolize the elements depending on how elaborate one's practice is, but for the energy to be effective and balanced, at least one symbol for each should be present. There are specific elemental associations for each herb, crystal or color, as well as for other natural objects. They could be Seashells to symbolize Water, Stones to symbolize Earth, Feathers to symbolize Air and small pinches of smoldering herbs as a symbol for Fire. When these associations are acknowledged and the assistance of these elements is formally requested, powerful spell works are created. To work with the elements successfully in both magic and ritual, one has to have a willingness to learn more about them and also develop an intuitive sense of your individual relationship with the essence of each elemental magic. You probably have an element that you associate well with more than the others already, so spend time exploring that connection. See where that takes you and then you can begin to work with the elements that have less personal resonance. As you continue to progress in your spiritual path, you will find that your understanding of the elements will be coming into balance progressively and easily. Read more about the elements from as many sources as possible and seek out your direction with them by interacting with them in nature and via magic. Each practitioner must learn and feel the elements. It can take time to get the hang of these elements and understand them, so personal study is required. The classical elements have been laid out conveniently – read them, learn about them and try to see them all around you.

Many Wiccans even go as far as meditating on the Elements. The knowledge of The Elements is very vital in herbal lore as well as the practice of Magick, the Wiccan magic practice.

THE EARTH ELEMENT

This element is most closely linked with our physical world and existence. It is also the densest of all the elements. It governs material existence, as well as money, property, business, security, loyalty, responsibility and everything related to the physical body and health, including finances. It is the feminine element of the mother goddess and symbolizes stability and growth. It is also the foundation on which the other elements move and is receptive energy that helps us accept responsibility. Earth is an elemental energy that brings our attention to the limitations in our makeup. Earth's season is usually in winter and its direction is the north. Earth's place in the natural environment is a cave that symbolizes shelter, the womb, rebirth, and the home of the ancient oracles. Other places that have been associated with the Earth element include Forests, valleys, and fields. It is no wonder that the Earth element governs the home and the areas of physical needs such as the bathroom, the dining room, and practical tasks.

Earth is the element of buildings, financial institutions, catering, gardening, farming, business and all things related to handiworks. Earth's energy is grounding. People with Earth personalities love to be surrounded by family and loved ones and can be quite tactile. They usually love the pleasure of the senses and have a healthy libido. Too much of the Earth element slows things down and makes progress slow, and too little of the elements causes an inability to take healthy risks or to branch out.

The deities usually associated with the Earth element are Gaia, Pan, and the horned god. Gaia is the ancient Greek goddess of the earth and was the first deity of the oracle at Delphi. In Greek mythology, the pan was a shepherd who represents the spirit of untamed nature. He was also an ancient god of wild things. The pagan horned god, also known as the lord of the woods, is the consort of the triple goddess. The Horned God represents sexuality and vitality and is usually depicted as half-man, half-animal. He is a hunter and has been identified with the sacrificed and hunted animal. According to Wiccans, the earth has been our home and our mother ever since we emerged from the great oceans.

THE AIR ELEMENT

Air is usually considered the realm of intellect, thought, and creation. Magically, the air is clear and uncluttered and is always moving. It happens to be a powerful tool for change and traveling and its magic includes instruction, freedom, obtaining knowledge, uncovering lies, discovering the truth, making decisions and so on. It can also develop psychic aspects among its many other uses. Air is a masculine element and its color is yellow since it belongs to the realm of the east and spring.

Air is represented in the forms of tossing objects into the wind, aromatherapy songs, music magic, and hiding things in high places. Air also rules the visualization. Its direction is the east and is usually symbolized by the sky, wind, breezes, clouds, feathers, breath, vibrations, smoke, plants, herbs, trees, and flowers. The zodiac signs associated with this element are Gemini, Libra and Aquarius. Being the most ethereal of all the elements, air rules the mind and all mental activities. The direction of the air is the east and is the element of the wind. Areas governed by the air are meeting rooms, schools, libraries, airports, railway stations, and bus terminals. The air element is connected with mathematics, science and the law and its places are the mountain tops, windy plains, clear or cloudy skies, and it presides over the eastern quarter of a room or building. People with the personalities of the earth element are always rational and analytical as they are clear thinkers and don't rush into things. Occasionally, they enjoy mental stimulation, good debates and an exchange of ideas. An abundance of the Air element creates a judgmental and critical outlook with a pedantic attitude towards all things. These personalities can put a damper on creative ideas in their early stages without any rational thinking. An overabundance of the air element can cause a person to live in a fantasy world and give in to ideas that have no substance. It causes them to approach things that are untenable and blinds them from pitfalls.

The deities usually associated with this element are Shu, Thoth, Hermes, and Mercury. Shu was the Egyptian god of the air who created the earth and the sky with Tefnut, his consort and goddess of moisture. Thoth was the Egyptian god of the moon and the god of wisdom. He kept secret knowledge.

THE FIRE ELEMENT

This element is often associated with the sun. The sun is considered to be the giver of life and therefore this element rules passion, intensity, desire, intuition, understanding, imagination and possibilities. Fire cleanses and purifies, but can also be destructive and creative. It can consume anything in its path, and as such, it is the only element that cannot exist without feeding on something else. Fire offers warmth and cooks food, but it could also get out of control and has the power to transform everything it comes in contact with. It rules the south and is often related to motivation, creativity as well as passion. It has a fast and forceful power and energy and is also uplifting and frightening when it goes out of control. It is a creative spark in everybody and promotes courage as well as strength in individuals. It helps us fight for want we want. People with the fire element personality are charming, charismatic and passionate, they live their lives to the fullest and rely heavily on their instincts and intuition. Their strengths tend to be creativity and leadership. Too much fire can be destructive because there are no limits, while an overabundance of fire leads to selfishness, self-centeredness and unrealistic expectations of others; too little or no fire leads to lack of energy or motivation.

THE WATER ELEMENT

Water represents emotions, absorptions, subconscious, purification, eternal movement, wisdom, the soul, the emotional aspects of love and feminity. In rituals, water is represented in the form of pouring water on objects, making concoctions, healing spells, ritual baths and throwing objects into water. Its color is the blue of the deep ocean, and it rules the sunset and dusk as well as the season of autumn.

For Wiccans, it was the birthplace where the ancestors first assembled. The energy of water rules the west and its season is autumn, it purifies, heals, offers emotional release and removes stagnation. Water personalities are spiritual, emotional, sensitive, and very intuitive. They approach life from a feeling perspective rather than a thinking one and are usually very spontaneous. Too little water makes them emotionally distant and creates in them an inability to express themselves. Too much water makes all the emotions extreme, which makes the day to day functioning if such a person difficult in the world and causes psychic overload.

The deities associated with water are Tiamat, Venus, Neptune, and Epona. Tiamat represents the chaos and energy of the ocean in Mesopotamian mythology. Tiamat is believed to be the primeval mother whose salt waters mingled with the water of apsu to initiate the creation of the gods. Neptune was the Roman god of the sea, and he had a fearful temper as his moods created storms.

In Greek mythology, Venus was the embodiment of love and beauty. It is believed that Venus was created by the foam of the sea and she had the ability to calm seas as well as ensuring the safety of voyages.

THE SPIRIT ELEMENT

The spirit element is usually referred to as Akasha in the Sanskrit language and pertains to the material plane. The element exists in the astral world. Ether was referred to as the quintessence in the Middle Ages, which meaning the fifth element. It is believed that the fifth element contained the secret of everlasting life and so ether was described as a substance that made up the heavens.

Various forms were used to express the qualities of the Spirit element, such as art, music, writing, magic, healing, religion, and ritual. This element is also associated with the crown chakra in the Tarot deck. The colors usually associated with this element are white or black as they are colors that reflect all other vibrations of light and dark.

The Spirit element is often very difficult to describe and is a force that is present everywhere and unites all things. It transports us beyond any narrow confines and allows us to open up to things much bigger and that go beyond thought and emotion. Unlike the other elements, the spirit element has no defined place or location and even though we cannot place it, we are aware of its omnipresent nature.

In Wicca, the five elements work together as a whole. At every significant occasion, Wiccans summon the elements because they form the basic emissaries that bring about fulfillment.

CHAPTER SUMMARY

This chapter is a detailed exposition of the five elements involved in the Wiccan practice and establishes their respective and collective significance in the performance of rituals and festivals.

CHAPTER FIVE.

WICCA AND THE SUMMERLAND

AFTER WICCA, WHAT NEXT?

The witches are firm believers in reincarnation, and they say that 'once a witch always a witch.'

Gerald Gardner

All religions of the world serve as an avenue for reaching unto the unknown via ways other than science. Although the beliefs vary from one religion or one sect to another and are dogmatic, they definitely form the basis on which their respective followers lead their lives. One of such vital questions that religion answers is on the topic of death and the life hereafter. What are the truths about death? Is death the end of an individual? If not, after death, what happens next? How valid are reincarnation, eternity, or eternal life and eternal damnation as preached by several religions? Is there a heaven or a hell, or any other places meant for similar purposes, awaiting mankind after death? The questions are definitely endless. However, just like many other world religions, Wicca has its distinctive, and of course, dogmatic beliefs and teachings about the afterlife.

WHAT IS THE WICCAN PERSPECTIVE ON DEATH?

Do Witches believe in death? Yes, but not as the end to life. Wiccans consider death a transition from the physical realm to a supernatural one. At death, it is the belief that people transition from their physical forms into ancestral bodies, which, though not physically present with humans, can be reached via rituals. This explains the depth of the Wiccan relationship with the dead. Wiccans hold that a deceased relative does not fall into oblivion, but passes into a separate state from which he can communicate with his descendants. Communication with the dead is possible, though not common, via means of dreams, whispers and quick glimpses. It is based on this belief that some Wiccans summon their ancestors to their personal rituals and festivals for purposes ranging from protection to provision and many others. For this class of Wiccans, the dead are placed right below the small deities, which come immediately after the Goddess and the God. In essence, death is not the end but a mere transition into another realm, which is believed to be more powerful and spiritually inclined than the physical realm.

But again, even among Wiccans, beliefs about the fate of the dead differ. While some other Wiccan groups agree that death isn't the end, they hold on the contrary that not everyone who dies automatically attains a position in the deity hierarchy. Some ancient Wiccan myths hold that there is a place designated for all the deceased. This place is differently referred to as the Underworld, the Otherworld and more commonly as the Summerland. Others believe that before they go into the Summerland, they are kept in an unknown space and that it is from this point, according to coven leaders like Raymond Buckland, that the souls which successfully learn the necessary lessons are liberated and promoted to the Summerland where they can be reached by living Wiccans through rituals.

As with many other beliefs in Wicca, opinions about the afterlife are predictably divergent. After all, it is the afterlife, who can be so sure? Despite the many differences, however, most Wiccan groups agree on a number of opinions about what happens to an individual after death.

NO HEAVEN, NO HELL

To start with, the concept of heaven has widened and grown beyond the Christian domain and is now being used as any pleasant destination after death. This said, I must mention that Wiccans do not believe in the Christian heaven, and of course, it goes without mention that the Christian heaven is too parochial to accommodate members of the neopagan religion. However, if we go by the definition of heaven as a strictly Christian creation, Wiccans do not believe in it. More so, it is not in any way Wiccan that there is a binary destination for departed souls based on their 'good' or 'bad' works. For Witches, there is neither heaven nor hell as the Christians claim. In other words, there are no such places where souls are damned to spend eternity. From a different perspective, however, if heaven is viewed more liberally as a place where souls congregate after death but do not necessarily have to remain there forever, the Wiccan heaven is the Summerland, but there's never a Wiccan hell. This does not imply that Wicca does not differentiate between good and bad, or good and evil as the case may be. As a matter of fact, it does, and this forms a fundamental pillar in its doctrines and principles. I shed more light on this under the final point in this list.

SUMMERLAND IS THE ULTIMATE DESTINATION

Again, care must be taken not to mistake the word 'ultimate' for 'eternal', which happens to be the general belief of Christianity and a couple of other religions. For Witches, life operates in a cycle, and the idea of eternity seems to disrupt the flow and put the soul in bondage. It is the common saying among Wiccans that once a Witch, always a Witch. This goes beyond the present life and does not imply that once a person becomes a Witch in a lifetime, they remain one till death. Instead, it means that the Wiccan life cycle goes beyond one particular lifetime and that upon death, a Wiccan does not stop being a Witch, but simply changes their physical form and comes back to life as a

Wiccan incarnate. Reincarnation is, therefore, a pivotal stage in the afterlife. For certain groups, this cycle is endless, which means an individual can reincarnate as many times as possible. This understanding forms the basis for the Wiccan belief that a Witch should not be forced to stay alive, especially when they are inflicted by an unyielding ailment or situation. They practice mercy killing when utmostly needed because they know that they are not necessarily killing the person but unleashing their souls to continue in the cycle. This also serves as a way of cheering up families of the deceased. More so, death is seen as a necessary part of the birth-death-rebirth circle. They celebrate deaths through what is known as the Summerland Rite, which involves the ushering of a soul into another plane of existence.

However, for certain covens, such as the Raymond Buckland-led group, there is an end to the reincarnation process, and by extension, the life cycle. This is the stage when a soul, upon death, sufficiently learns all the necessary lessons and, as a reward, is liberated from the cycle into the Summerland.

THE DEAD AREN'T REALLY DEAD

Another common afterlife belief among almost all Wiccan groups is that when a Wiccan dies, they are elevated into a state at which they can be reached by the living Wiccans for blessings, protection, and provision, among other benefits. Some Wiccans also invite the spirits of their ancestors to their rituals.

This is to place emphasis on the continuous existence of those who are dead. In other words, they are not actually dead but are living in another realm. They also believe that the supernatural realm is the Summerland. Although this is a fairly popular belief among Wiccan covens, a small sector disagrees to date. An example of such contrary opinions can be traced to a certain High Priest, Alex Sanders, who is credited with the statement, 'they are dead; leave them in peace'.

YOUR PRESENT LIFE INFLUENCES THE NEXT

Unlike many other religions in which the actions of an individual while on earth are judged at a specific place in the supernatural realm, in Wicca, a Witch's actions in the present life are rewarded or punished accordingly in the next life. For Wiccans, there is neither heaven nor hell, and as a result, all the good or bad that people do come back to them on earth, but in another lifetime. In addition, there is no end to existence, but there is no eternity in a special place other than the world. Hence, Wiccans place less emphasis on the afterlife and concentrate instead on making the best of the present life with the strong belief that whatever they make of this present life will haunt or help the next.

The topic of life hereafter is a sensitive one that has raised curiosity across time among the secular and nonsecular world — historians, scientists, astrologers, philosophers, religious leaders and scholars, and so many others. As interesting as the topic is, it has remained evasive and continues to manifest itself in multiple forms.

Owing to this, no group of religious scholars or leaders or secular researchers has been able to find a single convincing answer to the questions bugging the mind of the world over the ages. Even among religions of the world where there are claims about the afterlife, there has never been a consensus, and Wicca is not exempted from this situation.

Newer dimensions of answers about the afterlife continue to manifest over the ages so much that seeking a consensus of the divergent opinions is a fruitless endeavor. Thankfully enough, Wicca places individuality above communality. In addition to the general traditional beliefs, Witches are encouraged to trust the discoveries from their respective personal encounters with the Spirit world.

CHAPTER SUMMARY

What is the fate of the Witch after death? Do Wiccans believe in the afterlife? Find all the answers to the questions bordering life after now from the Wiccan perspective in this chapter.

CHAPTER SIX.

THE SCIENCE AND FICTION OF WICCA

Over the years, like every other religion in its developmental stage, Wicca has been confronted with several challenges. These clashes revolve around the authenticity of the religion. Many non-Wiccans have doubted the claims of Wiccan practice in almost every form. To this day, people continue to question the sanity of Wiccan rituals, festivals, and the belief system as a whole. This is not unexpected. Christianity, for example, some 2000 years ago faced its own challenges from Jews. Similarly, so many aspects of the Wiccan beliefs have been questioned both by scholars and members of other religions. In the middle of all these, Wicca has continued to expand in acceptance as more people continue to see the essence of the religion. In this chapter, I discuss two important confrontations that Wicca has suffered. They can be summarized as follows:

- Can the Wiccan beliefs and practices be backed by science?

- Why is Wicca so occultic if it is not a dangerous Satanist religion?

First off, to expect that religion is backed up by scientific facts is to deny it the dogmatic and spiritual nature of all religions of the world. Notwithstanding, as Wicca is not a full religion going by certain factors such as having a holy book or a specific day of worship, among others, it has some scientific backup. Wicca is scientific only to the extent that it believes in the vibrational energy of Witches and objects. According to Edwin Maccoy's 'Spellworks for Covens', the energy from a Witch's body operates on a vibration that has a scientific and spiritual dimension to it. The speed of the vibrations depends largely on the molecular movement within the body. More so, during the Wiccan rituals, it is the belief among Wiccans that the molecules from their physical and spiritual entities combine to form the energy required to carry out the rituals. This form of energy is also witnessed during meditation, when a body moves from a docile state to a frenzied and spiritually charged one. Another scientific dimension of Wicca lies in the fact that it draws energy from each of the four classic elements of nature — Air, Wind, Water, and Earth. The other element in the set, Spirit, is the only supernatural source of Wicca. This established that although Wicca is not pure science because it relies heavily on spirituality, it definitely draws on scientific sources for energy and, as a result, has enough scientific backup. Now, because of its highly occultic nature and I must admit that this is true of Wicca. It has drawn so many criticisms based on misinformation and misconceptions from non-Wiccans.

In the rest of this chapter, I discuss some of the most common misconceptions about Wicca. It is my belief that your doubts will be cleared if you also share similar prejudices against the religion.

"WICCA IS SATANIST IN NATURE"

This is perhaps the most common fundamental misinformation about Wicca. To put it most simply, Wiccans do not believe in nor worship any Devil, and neither do they plug into the Christian definition of Hell. For Witches, there is no Devil, who specializes in causing harm or wreaking havoc in the world as many people have been made to believe. This is not to say that Wiccans do not believe in the existence of evil spirits. As a matter of fact, they do and always ward off spirits with evil intents at every point of making rituals, festivals or meditation. More so, Wiccans believe in protecting themselves against negative spirits, but do not believe that there is an entity called Devil that masterminds the world's atrocities, as some other religions claim.

"WITCHES ARE DANGEROUS PEOPLE"

There is also the misconception that Witches are evil and dangerous people. This is ridiculously false. Like I already clarified in the initial section of this book, a difference must be made between 'Witch' (upper case) and 'witch' (lower case). The former is the title by which a disciple of Wicca is known. Witches live by the rede, which states that no Wiccan must do anything that would bring harm to anyone. They also operate on the Three-Fold Law, which holds that whatever you wish upon someone else would come back to you threefold. There is no doubting the fact that Witches have the power to cast evil spells or curses on people, but they do not harness their powers for negative purposes, neither do they use it to hurt people. It is therefore judgmental to use the negative connotation of the word 'witch' on Wiccans. Although most still prefer to be called Witches, some traditions have adopted the title 'Wiccans'.

"WICCANS MAKE SACRIFICES OF ANIMALS"

Do Wiccans make sacrifices? Yes! Do Wiccans make sacrifices using animals? No! Wiccans emphasize the value of nature and respect all living things. This is due, in part, to the fact that Wicca encourages animism. A typical Wiccan sacrifice involves items such as fruits, flowers, bread, and a few others but never animals nor any sacrifice involving blood. As a matter of fact, these items are not compulsory for personal sacrifices in Wicca, but only in formal rituals. In addition to the above false notions is the saying that Wicca is not a recognized religion. Although there are many boxes which Wicca does not tick, such as having a Holy Book, Wicca has grown to be recognized by some modern governments. In some areas such as New Jersey, US, the Wiccan holidays are recognized in the education calendar. The confusion is fueled by the occultic nature of Wicca and that it emphasizes individuality over commonality, hence there have been lots of alterations depending on the Wiccan traditions.

CHAPTER SUMMARY

This chapter dwells on the many misconceptions that trail Wicca as a religion. No thanks to its occultic nature. What you know about Wicca might just not be right. Discover the truths here.

CONCLUSION

WICCA AND YOU

Evaluating your Decision to be a Witch

The first time I called myself a 'Witch' was the most magical moment of my life.

Margot Adler

Y ou want to be a Witch, right? It is an excellent choice you have made. If you have been carefully following the organization of the Wiccan steps and processes in this book to this point, I congratulate you. There is no doubt that your abyss of ignorance about Wicca and Witchcraft has been filled to a great extent. The information provided in this book could have been overwhelming, hence there is no need to rush through the Wiccan practice.

Take it one step at a time. Meanwhile, I should state that this book is only a guide for you as a beginner. There is still a lot more to learn about Wicca, but, as they say, learning is more productive in practice. As you get to practice, you will understand and appreciate the individuality of Wicca and also unveil so many secrets for yourself. For the rest of this book, I provide very personal tips to help you fully understand the journey you are about to embark on.

DO YOU REALLY WANT TO BE A WITCH?

This is a quick call to help you check why you decided to be a Witch in the first place. Ensure you are under no influence whatsoever and that your decision has been thought through. This is not to scare you, but to ensure that you are really interested in being a Witch and completely committed to the cause. Your level of diligence in the Wiccan practice will depend largely on your drive. Be sure you are starting on the right foot.

ARE YOU READY TO LEARN?

Oh yes! Wicca requires a lot of readiness to learn. You cannot be lazy. You must be inquisitive enough to learn the ropes of Wicca if you must progress as a Witch.

A knowledge of rituals, festivals, holidays, spells, tarot cards, and meanings, incantations, herbs, crystals, candles and so many other key components of the practice will take you farther in Wicca, but you must be careful not to rush into learning them all.

BE SKEPTICAL BUT OPEN-MINDED

To be a successful Wiccan, you must be willing to break new grounds of knowledge. Do not passively swallow every dot of information you are given hook, line, and sinker. Actively engage and question the practices and beliefs, not as non-Wiccans, whose stock-in-trade is to doubt and water down the beliefs, but as a scholar who wishes to widen the scope of knowledge.

Remember the place of individual efforts. Ask valid questions and determine to build on what you have learned. Break new grounds. Challenge heresies!

DECIDE ON YOUR AREA OF FOCUS

You would have inevitably discovered that Wicca is broad, both in concept and in practice. To sufficiently practice Witchcraft, you cannot be the Jack of all skills. Determine which aspect you would love to focus on and concentrate fully. If you are going to focus on candle magic, determine that this is the case from the beginning so as not to waste your resources on acquiring the tools and supplies intended for others. On a final note, always remember that you are the most important factor in your Wiccan journey. Pay close attention to yourself and your intuition. Listen closely to your spirit at every point of making a decision, and you are bound to have a beautiful Wiccan experience. Also, bear in mind that it is not the path of a Witch to abuse their powers by doing evil to others. Whatsoever you do unto others will come back to you threefold.

Bide the Wiccan Law ye must,

In perfect love and perfect trust.

These eight words the Wiccan Rede fulfill,

And ye harm none do as ye will.

And ever mind the Rule of Three,

What ye send out comes back to thee.

Follow this with mind and heart,

And merry ye meet and merry ye part.

(The Wiccan Rede)

CPSIA information can be obtained
at www.ICGtesting.com
Printed in the USA
BVHW071829270421
605952BV00011B/666